INTRODUCING THE OLD TESTAMENT

ALSO BY JOHN F. FINK:

Moments in Catholic History

Travels With Jesus in the Holy Land

Married Saints

The Doctors of the Church of the First Millennium

The Doctors of the Church of the Second Millennium

American Saints

Future American Saints?

Letters to St. Francis de Sales: Mostly on Prayer

Jesus in the Gospels

Biblical Women

Saint Thomas More: Model for Modern Catholics

Patriotic Leaders of the Church

Memoirs of a Catholic Journalist

Mere Catholicism: What the Catholic Church Teaches and Practices

100 Important Events in Catholic History

The Mission and Future of the Catholic Press (Editor)

Visit our web site at
www.stpauls.us
or call 1-800-343-2522
and request current catalog

INTRODUCING THE OLD TESTAMENT

AN OVERVIEW OF ITS CONTENTS AND ITS MESSAGE

John F. Fink

ST PAULS

Library of Congress Cataloging-in-Publication Data

Fink, John F.
    Introducing the Old Testament: an overview of its contents and its message / John F. Fink.
        pages cm.
    ISBN 978-0-8189-1382-2
1. Bible. Old Testament–Introductions. I. Title.
    BS1140.3.F56 2015
    221.6'1–dc23
                        2015001533

Produced and designed in the United States of America by the
Fathers and Brothers of the Society of St. Paul,
2187 Victory Boulevard, Staten Island, New York 10314-6603
as part of their communications apostolate.

ISBN 978-0-8189-1382-2

Current Printing - first digit   1   2   3   4   5   6   7   8   9   1 0

Place of Publication:
2187 Victory Blvd., Staten Island, NY 10314 - USA

Year of Current Printing - first year shown

2015   2016   2017   2018   2019   2020   2021   2022   2023   2024

CONTENTS

INTRODUCTION

Did you ever notice on *Jeopardy!* that "The Bible" or "The Old Testament" is the last category chosen by the contestants? The people on that TV show are chosen because of their knowledge, but they realize their shortcomings when it comes to the Bible.

This is particularly true when it comes to the Old Testament. Far more Christians know the New Testament than the Old Testament – quite naturally since we are Christians, not Jews. Nevertheless, Christian churches have always insisted that both are important.

During the development of the Bible, one of the earliest controversies was started in the second century by Marcion, who rejected the Old Testament and refused to see any connection between it and the New Testament. However, St. Justin vehemently opposed Marcion because his conversion to Christianity came about because he was convinced that it was the fulfillment of the Old Testament prophecies.

The *Catechism of the Catholic Church* states that: "The Old Testament is an indispensable part of Sacred Scripture. Its books are divinely inspired and retain a permanent value, for the Old Covenant has never been revoked" (#121).

Also, "Christians venerate the Old Testament as the true Word of God. The Church has always vigorously opposed the idea of rejecting the Old Testament under the pretext that the New has rendered it void (Marcionism)" (#123).

And there's this: "Christians read the Old Testament in the light of Christ crucified and risen. Such typological reading discloses the inexhaustible content of the Old Testament; but it must not make us forget that the Old Testament retains its own intrinsic value as revelation reaffirmed by Our Lord himself. Besides, the New Testament has to be read in the light of the Old. Early Christian catechesis made constant use of the Old Testament" (#129).

Therefore, I have written this book about the Old Testament to encourage you to read and understand it. I hope you will read it along with me as I summarize the books.

I definitely will go into more detail about some of the books than others. For example, I'll cover Genesis and Exodus more thoroughly than the following three books. I'll spend more space on the historical books than on the fictional ones.

The Old Testament consists basically of the Jewish Scriptures, although Catholics recognize seven books that are not in the Jewish Scriptures. The Jews didn't include them in their canon because there were no copies in Hebrew when they decided on their canon. When Protestants compiled their Bibles in the sixteenth century, they accepted the Jewish canon. Today Protestant Bibles usually include those seven books in an Apocrypha section.

The Catholic Bible has forty-six books in the Old Testament. The Pentateuch (which the Jews call the Torah) consists of the first five books. The Catholic Bible follows those books with sixteen historical books, seven wisdom books, and eighteen prophetic books. Since this is the most complete Old Testament, and since I'm a Catholic, I plan to follow that arrangement.

However, I don't have forty-six chapters in this book. I don't have separate chapters for all of the Jewish minor prophets because I thought I should consider them in the context of Jewish history, and I tell about them there. I do have separate chapters on the major prophets, but they also are inserted where they fit in historically.

I encourage you to read this book while reading the Old Testament. Each of the chapters began in my weekly column in *The Criterion*, the newspaper for the Archdiocese of Indianapolis, and the series of columns took a full year. However, recognizing that not everyone is going to read it that slowly, I hope that you will come away with a better understanding of the Old Testament.

Biblical Abbreviations

OLD TESTAMENT

Genesis	Gn	Nehemiah	Ne	Baruch	Ba
Exodus	Ex	Tobit	Tb	Ezekiel	Ezk
Leviticus	Lv	Judith	Jdt	Daniel	Dn
Numbers	Nb	Esther	Est	Hosea	Ho
Deuteronomy	Dt	1 Maccabees	1 M	Joel	Jl
Joshua	Jos	2 Maccabees	2 M	Amos	Am
Judges	Jg	Job	Jb	Obadiah	Ob
Ruth	Rt	Psalms	Ps	Jonah	Jon
1 Samuel	1 S	Proverbs	Pr	Micah	Mi
2 Samuel	2 S	Ecclesiastes	Ec	Nahum	Na
1 Kings	1 K	Song of Songs	Sg	Habakkuk	Hab
2 Kings	2 K	Wisdom	Ws	Zephaniah	Zp
1 Chronicles	1 Ch	Sirach	Si	Haggai	Hg
2 Chronicles	2 Ch	Isaiah	Is	Malachi	Ml
Ezra	Ezr	Jeremiah	Jr	Zechariah	Zc
		Lamentations	Lm		

NEW TESTAMENT

Matthew	Mt	Ephesians	Eph	Hebrews	Heb
Mark	Mk	Philippians	Ph	James	Jm
Luke	Lk	Colossians	Col	1 Peter	1 P
John	Jn	1 Thessalonians	1 Th	2 Peter	2 P
Acts	Ac	2 Thessalonians	2 Th	1 John	1 Jn
Romans	Rm	1 Timothy	1 Tm	2 John	2 Jn
1 Corinthians	1 Cor	2 Timothy	2 Tm	3 John	3 Jn
2 Corinthians	2 Cor	Titus	Tt	Jude	Jude
Galatians	Gal	Philemon	Phm	Revelation	Rv

1

THE BOOK OF GENESIS

The Book of Genesis begins, "In the beginning." It really is about the beginning, and what is in it was chosen to provide the foundation for all that will follow.

The first eleven chapters discuss the time of creation and our earliest human ancestors while chapters twelve to fifty begin the stories of the Jewish patriarchs. The stories in the first part describe some sort of model, for good or bad, of the proper relationship of God to the world of humans.

Many of the stories are like others that are known to have existed in Mesopotamia. They are meant to tell us that God created all things and found them good and, although evil followed, goodness will prevail.

We should also keep in mind that Genesis had more than one author. It's a complex work and the final editor, whoever he might have been, used several sources and literary traditions. There are, for example, two accounts of the creation, one in the first chapter and the other in the second chapter.

Catholics and most other Christians do not believe that creation necessarily happened as either account states. Neither the Book of Genesis nor any other biblical book is a scientific treatise. Its message is theological, not scientific.

The message that the stories in these chapters tries to convey is that there is a tension between God's goodness to the earth and the human response of disobedience or sin.

The first three chapters tell the story of God's creation, which God saw was very good, but also the first human sin. The fourth and fifth chapters show how the evil of sin spread through the world.

God then decided that he must begin again, so he sent the great flood that drowned everyone except those in Noah's ark. The account in Genesis is almost identical to one of the stories in the ancient Babylonian poem *The Epic of Gilgamesh*. In that poem, though, the survivor of the flood was Utnapishtim rather than Noah, and Utnapishtim achieved immortality after the flood while Noah did not.

God then began again with Noah and his family, making a covenant with Noah that he would never again destroy the world by a flood. People again multiplied across the earth, but sin persisted.

There's a general pattern to these stories: God acts lovingly towards humanity, people disobey God and sin, God announces punishment, the punishment is given, and God ends with compassion by showing mercy and a new blessing.

Adam and Eve, Cain and Abel, the angels and the women (see the first part of chapter 6), the wicked generation of the flood, the sons of Noah, the people who build the tower of Babel, all were given signs of God's love and bountiful providence as they filled the earth. Yet each generation rose in disobedience.

Genesis also tries to give the genealogy from Adam to Noah and then from Noah to Abraham. The long ages attributed to the men are similar to the fantastic ages given to ten kings in Babylonian myths. We are then prepared for the arrival of Abraham.

Abram migrates to Canaan

Unlike the first 11 chapters of Genesis, chapters 12 to 50 are set in historical times. They are set in Mesopotamia, Palestine and Egypt. The persons engage in actions typical of 1900 to 1500 B.C. The stories are similar to oral lore of tribal groups. And the purpose of the stories is to trace the direct tribal and clan ancestors of Israel.

We meet the great patriarch Abraham (or Abram until his name is changed), who is claimed as their father in faith by the Muslims as well as by Jews and Christians. In obedience to God's command and his promise to make him a great nation, he, his wife Sarai, and his nephew Lot migrated from Mesopotamia to the land of Canaan.

Abram and Lot were rich in livestock, silver and gold. They were nomads who pitched their tents in several places in Canaan, beginning with Shechem (modern Nablus). When a famine struck the land, they continued down to Egypt.

As they were entering Egypt, Abram told Sarai to pass herself off as his sister. If the Egyptians knew that she was his wife, he reasoned, they might kill him so they could have her. However, when the Egyptians saw how beautiful Sarai was, they praised her to the Pharaoh, who took her into his palace.

When Pharaoh learned that Sarai was actually Abram's wife, he gave her back to him and ordered him to leave. They returned to Canaan. Then, realizing that he and Lot had too many livestock for the land to support, Abram suggested that they separate. Lot chose to live in Sodom at the bottom of the Dead Sea, and Abram settled in Hebron, west of the Dead Sea.

Chapter 14 reports a war involving four kings, during which Lot was taken prisoner. When Abram learned of it, he organized a rescue party that defeated the kings and recovered Lot and all of his possessions.

When he returned, he was met by Melchizedek, identified as king of Salem and also a priest. He blessed Abram and Abram, in turn, gave Melchizedek a tenth of everything he owned.

The Letter to the Hebrews in the New Testament tells us that Melchizedek is a type of Christ. Since the Bible doesn't say anything about Melchizedek's ancestry or his death, the letter concluded that he resembled the Son of God and remains a priest forever. Jesus was, the letter says, a priest forever according to the order of Melchizedek rather than according to the Jewish order of Aaron.

God then appeared to Abram in a vision and promised him that his descendants would be as numerous as the stars in the sky and that they would populate the land from Egypt to the Euphrates River, then occupied by people from ten tribes.

God also told Abram that his descendants would be aliens and enslaved and oppressed for 400 years, thus alerting us to the events of the Book of Exodus.

There was, though, an obvious problem here: Abram and Sarai were in their 80s and they had no children.

Ishmael and Isaac

Chapter 16 of Genesis tells us about the birth of Ishmael. Since Abram and Sarai had no children, Sarai gave her Egyptian maidservant Hagar to Abram as his concubine. But after Hagar became pregnant there was great friction between her and Sarai. (Wow, imagine that. Just because Hagar was bearing Abram's son?)

Anyway, Sarai made life so difficult for Hagar that she ran away. But God found her and sent her back, telling her to submit to the abusive treatment.

Ishmael was born. He grew up to become the father of twelve sons, who are named in chapter 25. They became chieftains of twelve tribes and Ishmael is considered the father of the Arab nations.

But God told Abram that, despite their old ages, he and Sarai would have a son. In chapter 17 he made a covenant with Abram, changing his name to Abraham and Sarai's to Sarah. He also ordered, as a sign of the covenant, that all of his male descendants should be circumcised. This, of course, also applied to Ishmael's descendants.

One day three men appeared near Abraham's tent. He made them welcome and had Sarah prepare a meal for them. One of the men, whom Abraham realized was the Lord, told him that Sarah would have a child within a year. Sarah overheard the conversation and laughed since Abraham was now 100 years old and she was 90.

Of course, Sarah did become pregnant and bore Isaac. When he grew up and was playing with Ishmael, Sarah demanded that Hagar and Ishmael be sent away.

Sodom and Gomorrah

That didn't happen, though, until chapter 21 because chapters 18-20 tell us about the destruction of Sodom and Gomorrah. Genesis makes it clear that God destroyed Sodom because of homosexual sins and our word "sodomy" resulted from that.

Abraham's nephew Lot lived in Sodom. Two angels visited him and he offered them hospitality. When the townspeople learned about it, they demanded that Lot "bring them out to us that we may have intimacies with them" (Gn 19:5). When the men tried to storm the house, the angels kept them from reaching the doorway.

The angels then told Lot, his wife and two daughters to escape because God had sent them to destroy the city. Don't look back, they said. They escaped as a sulphurous fire destroyed Sodom and Gomorrah. But Lot's wife looked back and was turned into a pillar of salt.

Genesis then tells a story to ridicule their rival nations. Lot and his daughters settled in the hill country. The daughters plotted to have children by Lot since there weren't any other men around. For two nights they made him drunk and took turns having sex with him without his knowledge (if you can believe that).

The older daughter's son was named Moab, the ancestor of the Moabites, and the younger daughter's son was named Ammon, the ancestor of the Ammonites. It's the Bible's way of saying that those people came from an incestuous relationship.

Abraham's test

Chapter 22 of Genesis tells us the story of God's testing of Abraham, ordering him to kill his son Isaac as a sacrifice to prove the firmness of Abraham's faith. It should be noted that the Muslims, too, have this story. However, the Muslims believe that Abraham was ordered to sacrifice Ishmael.

Abraham, Isaac and two servants traveled for three days to Mount Moriah, which is in Jerusalem. Abraham and Isaac then climbed to the summit, with the wood for the holocaust on Isaac's shoulders. At one point, Isaac asked where the sheep for the holocaust was and Abraham replied that God would provide.

When they reached the summit, Abraham bound Isaac and put him on a large rock that served as the altar. We aren't told if Isaac resisted. Then Abraham took his knife and was about to slaughter his son when an angel called from heaven and told him to stop. He had passed the test.

The Jews and Muslims alike believe that the rock upon which Abraham was going to sacrifice Isaac (or Ishmael) is in the magnificent Dome of the Rock on the Temple Mount in Jerusalem. Solomon built his Temple over the rock and the Second Temple was there during the time of Christ. It was destroyed by the Romans in 70 A.D.

Muslims also believe that Muhammad ascended to heaven from the rock. The present Dome of the Rock was built by Caliph Abd al-Malik from 687 to 691.

Chapter 23 begins with Sarah's death when she was 127. Abraham purchased a cave for her tomb. When Abraham died at age 175, Isaac and Ishmael buried him in the cave. That tomb is in modern Hebron and I've visited it several times, although

pilgrims seldom go there these days because of the political un-
rest. Besides Abraham and Sarah, Isaac and Rebekah, and Jacob
and Leah are also buried there.

Isaac marries Rebekah

When it was time for Isaac to marry, Abraham didn't want
him to marry a Canaanite woman. So he sent his senior servant
back to his land in Mesopotamia (modern Iraq) to find a suitable
wife for Isaac. Chapter 24 tells the story. The servant traveled
back. As he stopped at a well, he prayed for a sign from God: If
a young woman came to draw water and he asked her for a drink,
and if she replied that she would water his camels, too, that would
be the woman he was seeking.

Of course, that happened. Rebekah, described as very beautiful, who turned out to be Abraham's grandniece, did exactly
that. Rebekah's brother Laban then made the servant welcome
and the servant told Laban about his mission. Rebekah agreed
to go to Canaan and become Isaac's wife.

Chapter 25 reveals that Abraham wasn't monogamous.
Besides Sarah and Hagar, he also had children by a concubine
named Keturah. However, when he died, he deeded everything
to Isaac. For his sons by concubinage, he made grants while he
was still living but then sent them away from Isaac.

Love story of Jacob and Rachel

Chapters 27-29 of Genesis tell us the great love story
between Jacob and Rachel, but it begins with dishonesty and
trickery. When reading it, we must remember that the story is

meant to show how God's promise to Abraham and Isaac continued through Jacob.

It's not a pious biography of a saint, but rather a saga about Israel's ancestors. The ancient readers would see Jacob as clever and wise.

There are also some sexual practices in this story that we definitely would not approve of today.

Esau and Jacob were the twin sons of Isaac and Rebekah, but Esau was the older. When they grew up, Isaac preferred Esau because he was a skilled hunter, but Rebekah liked Jacob better. (It sounds like a Smothers Brothers' routine.)

The trickery began when Isaac was a blind old man. He wanted to pass on his birthright to Esau, his older son, and told him that he would do so after Esau caught some game and made an appetizing dish for him.

Rebekah overheard the conversation. She got some of Esau's clothing and fixed Jacob up so that he felt hairy, as Esau was. She prepared a dish she knew Isaac liked and Jacob took it to his father before Esau returned. Isaac gave his blessing to Jacob, making him his heir and master over Esau.

When Esau learned of the trick, he resolved to kill Jacob. Rebekah saved Jacob by convincing Isaac to send Jacob off to his uncle Laban back in Mesopotamia, where Isaac and Rebekah had met. There Jacob met Rachel, Laban's daughter, who ran off quickly to tell Laban that Rebekah's son arrived. Laban immediately took Jacob in.

Rachel was "well-formed and beautiful" (Gn 29:17), and Jacob fell in love with her. He told Laban that he would work for him for seven years if he could have Rachel in marriage. Laban agreed and Jacob worked for him for seven years.

Laban, though, had an older daughter, Leah. During the wedding ceremony, the bride was veiled. That night the couple consummated their marriage in the dark. The next day Jacob discovered that he had been tricked and that he had married Leah.

Laban simply explained that it was not the custom in that country to marry off a younger daughter before an older one. However, he then proposed that Jacob marry Rachel, too, in return for another seven years of work for Laban. Jacob agreed, and thus he was married to both Leah and Rachel.

It happened that Leah was quite fertile, but Rachel was not. Leah began having children while Rachel remained barren. So Rachel gave her maidservant to Jacob, and the maidservant had a son. Then Leah ceased to bear children, and she, too, gave her maidservant to Jacob, and she, too, had a son. But then Leah became fertile again and bore two more sons, plus a daughter, Dinah. Finally, Rachel had two sons, Joseph and Benjamin. Thus Jacob had twelve sons and a daughter by four women.

Jacob returns to Canaan

From the middle of chapter 30 through chapter 35, the Book of Genesis tells about Jacob's decision to return to his homeland, where his father Isaac still lived.

Jacob worked for his uncle Laban, the father of Jacob's wives Leah and Rachel, for twenty years. By that time, Laban's attitude toward Jacob changed and they started to have serious disagreements. God told Jacob it was time for him to return to Canaan.

Genesis tells us how he had to outwit Laban to get away from him, but eventually he, Leah, Rachel and their children made their escape with Jacob's cattle, herds of sheep, and camels.

Laban chased after them, caught up with them, and demanded the return of his daughters and grandchildren. Finally, though, the two men made a pact, Laban kissed his daughters and grandchildren good-bye, and allowed them to continue their journey.

One night Jacob had a wrestling match with another man, who turned out to be an angel. During the match the angel wrenched Jacob's hip socket and, the Bible passage says, that explains why the Jews do not eat the sciatic muscle that is on the hip socket.

Jacob prevailed in the wrestling match and in the morning the angel changed his name to Israel "because you have contended with divine and human beings and have prevailed" (Gn 32:29). Later God appeared to him and confirmed the name change.

As Jacob and his huge contingent neared where his brother Esau lived in Edom, located south of the Dead Sea, he sent messengers ahead. The messengers returned, though, with the report that Esau was coming to meet Jacob with 400 men.

Jacob, naturally, was frightened. He planned to appease Esau with numerous camels, goats, sheep and cattle. However, after all those years, Esau's anger had cooled and the reunion was peaceful. Jacob and his family continued to Shechem, north of the Dead Sea.

Now Genesis gives us one of many salacious passages in the Bible. During the journey, Jacob's daughter Dinah went to visit some of the women of the land. While she was there, a man named Shechem (the same name as the city) raped her. Then he decided he wanted to marry her and sent his father to negotiate with Jacob.

Jacob's sons said that they could not give their sister to an uncircumcised man but would do so if all the men in the village would be circumcised. The men actually agreed, and then, while they were in pain after the circumcisions, Jacob's sons massacred all the men, sacked the city, and seized all their flocks, herds and women. Not everything in Genesis is a pious story.

During their journey, Rachel was pregnant again. As they neared Bethlehem, she went into labor. She bore another son, Benjamin, but she died in childbirth and was buried there. Today Rachel's Tomb in Bethlehem is one of the most popular Jewish shrines, especially for expectant mothers.

Jacob, now named Israel, settled in the land of Canaan with his twelve sons.

The story of Judah and Tamar

Before I write about the great masterpiece in Genesis about Joseph and his brothers, let me cover chapter 38, which is inserted in the story but has nothing to do with Joseph. It's an important chapter, though, for several reasons.

It tells the story of Judah, one of Jacob's sons, who married a Canaanite woman with whom he had three sons – Er, Onan and Shelah. When Er grew up, he married a woman named Tamar.

Then Er died. Jacob told Onan to marry Tamar, following the ancient Israelites' "law of the levirate" that required the deceased man's brother to have children with the widow to preserve the deceased man's line.

That law still existed in New Testament time when Sadducees questioned Jesus about the resurrection of the body by using the law of the levirate. In their test of Jesus, they said that seven brothers married the woman and asked whose wife she would be at the resurrection. (See Mt 22:23-33.)

Onan married Tamar. However, knowing that any children they had would be considered his brother's and not his, "whenever he had relations with his brother's widow, he wasted his seed on the ground, to avoid contributing offspring for his brother" (Gn 38:9). Because that act greatly offended God, Genesis says, the Lord took his life, as he had done to Er.

One of the reasons sometimes given for the Catholic Church's condemnation of contraception was this so-called "sin of Onan," although in this case it seems that God took his life because of Onan's violation of the law of the levirate rather than the means he used.

Judah, fearing that his third son, Shelah, might also die if he married Tamar, told Tamar to remain a widow. Years passed and Judah's wife died.

One day Tamar learned that Judah was going someplace, so she veiled her face and sat by the roadside. Jacob thought she was a harlot and propositioned her. He promised her a kid from his flock if she would have intercourse with him. She agreed, provided that Judah would leave his seal, cord and staff as a pledge until she received the kid.

Later, when Judah tried to send the kid, the prostitute could not be found.

Three months later, Judah learned that Tamar was pregnant. Indignantly, he demanded that she be brought out and burned. Then Tamar sent word to her father-in-law that she was with child by the man whose seal, cord and staff she displayed. Judah conceded that Tamar was more in the right than he was.

When Tamar gave birth, she had twins whom she named Perez and Zerah.

This episode is important because the Gospel According

to Matthew begins with the genealogy of Jesus and it includes this line: "Judah became the father of Perez and Zerah, whose mother was Tamar" (1:3).

Tamar is one of four women in the genealogy (the others are Rahab, Ruth and Bathsheba), all of whom were considered aliens by the Israelites and who bore sons in strange and unexpected ways.

The story of Joseph and his brothers

Chapters 37 through 50 of Genesis tell the story of Joseph and I hope you'll read them because the story is a masterpiece. It tells how divine providence brings about a totally unexpected end, how Joseph's brothers' plan to kill him leads to the Israelites' ancestors moving to Egypt.

As you read those chapters, note that every step along the way leads to the next, like the cleverly constructed plot of a piece of fiction. There were, in fact, two versions of the Joseph story. As *The Catholic Study Bible* says, "Some genius has taken the old themes and separate traditions and created a literary work of art, the earliest such masterwork that we know anywhere."

The two versions are known as the Yahwist and the Elohist sources. The Yahwist, written in Judah in the ninth or tenth century B.C., used the name *Yahweh* for God. The Elohist, written in Israel after Solomon's kingdom fell apart, used the name *Elohim* for God. (The Old Testament also has the Deuteronomist and the priestly sources.)

You can spot the two sources. When Joseph's father is called Israel, it's the Yahwist source; when he's called Jacob, it's the Elohist source. In one story, Reuben tries to save Joseph; in the other, it's Judah. In one source, Joseph is sold to Ishmaelites; in the other, it's to Midianites. In the Yahwist source, Joseph's coat causes the brothers' jealousy; in the Elohist source, it's Joseph's dreams. There are also two parallel accounts of the brothers' journeys to and from Egypt.

With that background, I'll get started on the story, although it'll be only a Cliffs Notes version. Please do read the whole thing, although you can do it a chapter at a time rather than all at once.

It can be said that the Israelite patriarchs and matriarchs were terrible parents. They had favorites among their children and let them know it. Rebekah favored Jacob while Isaac favored Esau. Now we learn that Jacob (Israel) loved Joseph best of all his 12 sons. Can you imagine why Joseph's brothers might have been jealous?

Of course, Joseph didn't help his cause. He told his brothers about a couple of his dreams in which it appeared that the brothers would be bowing down before him.

One day ten of the brothers (all except Benjamin, the youngest) were tending their sheep. Israel, blissfully unaware of how his sons felt about Joseph, sent Joseph after them. They saw him coming and planned to kill him until Reuben suggested that they just throw him into an empty cistern.

Soon a caravan of Midianites (or Ishmaelites) came by and Judah suggested that they sell Joseph as a slave to them. The deal was made for 20 pieces of silver. Then they took Joseph's long tunic and dipped it into the blood of a slaughtered goat so they could tell their father that Joseph was killed by a wild animal.

The Midianites took Joseph to Egypt and sold him to Potiphar, Pharaoh's chief steward.

Joseph confronts his brothers in Egypt

Joseph got along well with Potiphar, so well, in fact, that he was put in charge of his whole household. But Joseph was handsome, and soon Potiphar's wife took notice. She tried to get him to sleep with her, but he refused.

"She tried to entice him day after day" (30:10), with no success. On one occasion Joseph fled the house. The spurned woman then told Potiphar that Joseph had tried to lie with her. Enraged, Potiphar threw Joseph into the prison where royal prisoners were confined. Joseph soon made friends with the chief jailer.

Later, Pharaoh's royal cupbearer and chief baker angered him and were thrown into prison. They each had a dream and Joseph interpreted its meaning – that the cupbearer would be restored to his position and the baker killed. That's what happened.

Two years passed. Pharaoh had a dream, and then a second. He called the magicians and sages together and asked them to interpret the dreams. When none could do so, the cupbearer told Pharaoh about his experience with Joseph.

Joseph was brought into Pharaoh's presence and asked to interpret the dream. He replied that it wouldn't be he but God who would give Pharaoh the right answer.

After Pharaoh described his dreams (in chapter 41), Joseph told him that both of them indicated that Egypt would have seven years of abundance followed by seven years of famine. He suggested that Pharaoh seek a wise man and put him in charge of the land so he could appoint overseers who would store the food during the seven good years.

Pharaoh was so impressed that he put Joseph in charge of the whole land of Egypt, second in rank only to Pharaoh. He also gave him in marriage to Asenath, daughter of an Egyptian priest. Joseph was then thirty years old.

During the next seven years, Joseph saw to it that food products were stored throughout Egypt. He and Asenath also had two sons, Manasseh and Ephraim. When the famine began, Pharaoh told the people to go to Joseph, who rationed the food that had been stored.

The famine affected Canaan, too. When Jacob learned that there was food in Egypt, he sent his ten sons (all except Benjamin) down to procure some. Joseph, of course, immediately recognized them, but concealed his own identity and spoke to them through an interpreter. He accused them of being spies and threw them into prison.

After three days, he told them that one of them must remain in prison until the others returned with their youngest brother. Talking among themselves, and not realizing that Joseph could understand them, they said that they were being punished for what they did to Joseph.

Leaving Simeon behind, they returned home with food. When they emptied their sacks, they discovered the money they had taken for payment.

The Israelite ancestors migrate to Egypt

When Jacob learned, at the end of chapter 42 of Genesis, that the man who gave his sons food demanded that Benjamin be brought to Egypt before he would release Simeon from prison, he refused. But eventually food ran low again, and he felt compelled to allow it.

This time the brothers were met graciously, even invited to

have dinner with Joseph, although he still concealed his identity. He asked about his aged father and was so filled with emotion when he saw Benjamin that he had to hurry from the room.

But Joseph wasn't quite finished punishing his brothers. After loading them up with as much food as they could take back with them, he ordered his steward to put their moneybags with the grain and also to hide a silver goblet in Benjamin's bag. After they had gone, he sent the steward after them.

When he caught them, he said that, if he found the goblet in one of their bags, that one would die. Of course, he found it in Benjamin's. All the brothers returned to the city.

Then Judah appealed to Joseph, still not knowing it was Joseph. After a lengthy speech in which he told the story of what had happened, he asked to become the man's slave and to allow Benjamin to return to his father.

Joseph could restrain himself no longer. He revealed himself to his dumbstruck brothers. He told them that it was God's plan for saving lives that he sent him ahead of them to Egypt: "It was not really you but God who had me come here" (45:8).

He then told them that there were still to be five more years of famine, so it would be best for Jacob to come to Egypt. The brothers returned home and recounted to Jacob all that had happened. "It is enough," said Israel. "My son Joseph is still alive! I must go and see him before I die" (45:28).

On the way, Jacob stopped at Beersheba. There God appeared to him in a vision, telling him not to be afraid to go to Egypt. "Not only will I go down to Egypt with you; I will also bring you back here, after Joseph has closed your eyes" (46:4).

So Jacob, all of his sons and their wives and children migrated to Egypt – 66 persons in all. Adding Joseph, his wife and two sons, who were already in Egypt, this totaled seventy persons in all. Pharaoh told Joseph to settle them in the pick of the land, so they settled in the land of Goshen.

Jacob lived in Egypt for seventeen years, until his death at age 147. Before his death, he made Joseph promise to take his body back to Canaan and bury it in the cave where Abraham, Sarah, Isaac, Rebekah and Leah were already buried. Joseph did so, taking with him Jacob's family plus all the senior members of Pharaoh's court.

Joseph returned to Egypt and lived there until his death at age 110.

2

THE BOOK OF EXODUS

The Book of Genesis ends with Jacob (also called Israel) and his family, seventy people, in Egypt. The Book of Exodus begins there, but almost 400 years later – roughly twice the length of the history of the United States. The Israelites proliferated so much that Egypt's Pharaoh thought it prudent to stop their increase in case they would join Egypt's enemies in a war.

He enslaved the Israelites, forcing them to build the Egyptian cities. He also instructed midwives to kill the Israelite babies when they were born. Although the midwives disobeyed this order, the lives of Israelite boys were in danger.

Therefore, when Moses was born, his mother hid him for three months. Then she put him in a basket among reeds in the Nile River. Moses' sister Miriam watched to see what would happen. Pharaoh's daughter came with her attendants to bathe and they discovered the baby. Miriam asked if she should find an Israelite mother to nurse the boy and Pharaoh's daughter agreed. So Moses' mother nursed him until he was weaned. Then Pharaoh's daughter adopted him.

When Moses was about forty, he saw an Egyptian striking an Israelite. In anger, Moses killed the Egyptian. When this became known, Pharaoh sought Moses to put him to death, so

Moses fled Egypt for Midian, to the east of the Sinai Peninsula. There he married Zipporah and they had two children, Gershom and Eliezer.

A long time passed and the Pharaoh who sought Moses died.

One day, while Moses was tending the flock of his father-in-law, he saw a bush on fire, but the fire didn't consume it. When he went to investigate this phenomenon, God called out to him from the bush. He told Moses that he had chosen him to lead the Israelites out of Egypt and back to the land he had promised to Abraham, Isaac and Jacob.

When Moses asked who he was, God said, "I am who am." He told Moses that he could tell the Israelites, "I AM sent me to you" (3:14).

Moses argued with God, saying that Pharaoh wouldn't listen to him, and, besides, he was slow of speech. God said that he would perform wondrous deeds and he performed some signs, like turning Moses' staff into a snake and making his hand leprous and then clean again. He also told him that Moses' brother Aaron would be his assistant.

So Moses and his family returned to Egypt. He told Aaron what God had told him and the two men gathered the elders of the Israelites. They performed the signs that God put into his power, so the people believed.

Then they went to see Pharaoh, asking first that he let the Israelites go a three-days' journey to celebrate a feast. Pharaoh refused, as God had told Moses he would. He not only refused, but he ordered the foremen of the Israelites to make them work harder – to gather straw for the bricks they made instead of having it supplied to them.

It was time for Moses to return to Pharaoh.

Moses leads the Israelites out of Egypt

Chapters 7 to 12 tell about the ten plagues that God sent upon the Egyptians to convince Pharaoh to let the Israelites leave Egypt. Before each one, Moses and his brother Aaron told Pharaoh that the plague would occur and each time Pharaoh promised to release the Israelites if the plague was lifted. But each time, except the last, he reneged on his promise.

The ten plagues were: the Nile River and other water supplies turned into blood; frogs covering the land; gnats infesting humans and animals; swarms of flies everywhere; a severe pestilence that killed livestock; boils that afflicted the people; a hailstorm with lightning that killed all people and animals in the open and destroyed every growing thing; locusts that devoured whatever the hail hadn't destroyed; darkness that covered the land for three days; and the death of every first-born person or beast.

While the Egyptians suffered those plagues, the Israelites did not.

Prior to the tenth plague, the killing of the first-born, the Lord had Moses instruct the people how they were to prepare the Passover feast and then mark the doorposts of their homes with blood from a lamb. Seeing the blood, he said, he would "pass over" that house while he was killing the Egyptians.

This passage, from chapter 12, is read in Catholic churches worldwide during services on Good Friday.

The Israelites were instructed to keep that day as a memorial feast and a perpetual institution, which they do.

When the Egyptians discovered all of their eldest children dead, Pharaoh not only permitted the Israelites to leave, he chased them out. The Egyptian people gave them silver, gold and clothing and rushed them out before they could even prepare food for the journey.

The Bible says that the Israelites comprised about 600,000 men, not counting children – plus numerous flocks and herds. They had grown from the seventy people who arrived in Egypt 430 years earlier.

But they weren't safe yet. Pharaoh, suddenly realizing that all those slaves were leaving, again changed his mind. This time he sent his army – horses, chariots and charioteers – after the Israelites. They caught up with them at the Red Sea (or, perhaps, the Sea of Reeds).

We know what happened next because it has been dramatized in movies and TV series. But read chapter 14 to see how the Bible describes the event.

First, God's angel put a dark cloud between the Egyptians and the Israelites. Then, at God's command, Moses split the sea in two. During the night a strong wind turned the bottom into dry land. In the morning the Israelites marched through the sea, "with the water like a wall to their right and to their left" (14:22).

When the Egyptians followed, Moses stretched his hand over the sea and it drowned Pharaoh's entire army. "Thus the Lord saved Israel on that day from the power of the Egyptians" (14:30).

But now what were they to do?

God makes his covenant with the Israelites

After the Israelites crossed the Red Sea and escaped from Egypt, God led them into the desert of Sinai. They would be there for forty years, during which time all those who left Egypt would die except Joshua and Caleb. During those years, too, they lived with all the hardships associated with living in a desert.

Time after time they grumbled against Moses because of the lack of food and water. But God provided. Each morning he sent down manna, a dew that turned into flakes like hoarfrost when it evaporated. "It was like coriander seed, but white, and it tasted like wafers made with honey" (Ex 17:31). Each morning except on the Sabbath, for forty years, the people gathered manna. They gathered twice as much on the day before the Sabbath because the manna wasn't there on the Sabbath.

For meat, God rained down quail on the camp (and we presume that they ate the livestock they took with them). For water, he had Moses strike a rock and water flowed from it.

After traveling for two months, they came to Mount Sinai (sometimes called Mount Horeb). We aren't sure which mountain on the Sinai Peninsula that was. Many people are convinced that it's where the Greek Orthodox St. Catherine's Monastery has existed since the sixth century.

Here, in chapters 19-24 of the Book of Exodus, is where God made his covenant with the Jewish people. "If you hearken to my voice and keep my covenant," he said, "you shall be my special possession, dearer to me than all other people, though all the earth is mine" (19:5). In return, the people were to keep his commandments.

Through Moses, God delivered his Commandments. They are in chapter 20, verses 2-17. Reading them there, it's easy to see how the precise division of the precepts into ten was somewhat arbitrary and why Catholics and other Christians number them differently.

But God didn't deliver just Ten Commandments. Chapters

21-23 give many rules concerning slaves, personal injury, property damage, loans, social laws, religious laws, and much more, all part of the covenant. Those laws give us a good picture of what life was like among the Jewish people when the Bible was compiled.

One of the laws is, "You shall not boil a kid in its mother's milk" (23:19). This is the basis for the kosher law that forbids Jews to eat meat and dairy products at the same meal.

Then, in chapters 25-31, God proceeded to tell Moses how to construct the Ark of the Covenant that would contain the tablets of the Commandments, and its furnishings. That's followed with detailed instructions on how Aaron and his sons were to offer sacrifices on behalf of the Israelites.

After the Israelites ratified the covenant by agreeing to do what God told them, God invited Moses to ascend Mount Sinai where he would give him the stone tablets with the Ten Commandments, written by God himself. Moses ascended the mountain, where he stayed for forty days and forty nights.

With Moses away the Israelites sin

After forty days and nights, the Israelites didn't know what had happened to Moses, so they asked Aaron to make them an image of God. Aaron collected gold earrings, melted the gold and fashioned a golden calf. He then built an altar for the calf. The people made sacrifices to the calf and started to celebrate.

On Mount Sinai, God knew what had happened and told Moses that he would destroy the Israelites, who already had broken their covenant with him. But Moses pleaded with God on behalf of the people and God relented.

Then Moses descended the mountain, carrying the stone

tablets. When he caught sight of the golden calf and the people dancing, he became so angry that he threw the tablets down and broke them on the base of the mountain. He took the calf, fused it in a fire, ground it down to powder, and scattered it on the stream that flowed down Mount Sinai.

That wasn't all. He also called the Levites and ordered them to go through the camp and slay with their swords those who were especially guilty of the idolatry. They killed three thousand people.

The next day Moses went back up the mountain and asked God's forgiveness for the people's grave sin. God replied that he would punish the people for their sin when it was the right time to do so. He then told Moses that he was to lead the Israelites to the land he swore to give to Abraham, Isaac and Jacob, where they would drive out the six tribes living there.

Moses again remained on Mount Sinai for forty days. He cut two new stone tablets on which he wrote the Ten Commandments. When he returned to the camp, his face was so radiant that the people couldn't look at him. He had to put a veil over his face. He wore it except when he went into the meeting tent to converse with God.

Chapters 35-38 of the Book of Exodus report the construction of the Ark of the Covenant, the table on which it was to sit, the lampstand, the altar of incense, the altar of holocausts, and the court. All these were constructed under the supervision of a man named Bezalel and his assistant Oholiab.

The Ark was made of acacia wood, 45 inches long, 27 inches wide, and 27 inches high. The inside and outside were plated with gold, and a molding of gold was put around it.

Chapter 39 describes the elaborate vestments in which

Aaron and his sons were to be clothed as they performed their priestly duties.

When all was prepared, chapter 40 reports on the erection of the dwelling, including the placement of the Commandments in the Ark.

3

THE BOOK OF LEVITICUS

The Levites (descendants of Jacob's son Levi) were the tribe from which Israel's priests were drawn. Therefore, it's understandable that the Book of Leviticus, the third of the five books in the Jewish Torah, came from a priestly source.

We all know about the Ten Commandments, but there are really 613 commandments in the Torah, and 247 of them are in Leviticus. (No, I didn't count them, but someone apparently did.) So this is a book of laws supposedly handed down by God to Moses but actually compiled over a considerable amount of time after 538 B.C. Jewish scholars have debated the meaning of the laws ever since.

The basis for all these laws is that God is holy and there's a gulf between him and humans. However, there are moments when we enter into the realm of the sacred, especially when it comes to sexuality, birth and death.

Why should Christians be interested in these ancient Jewish laws, especially after St. Paul taught us that Christians are free from the Mosaic Law? One reason would be to gain a better understanding of parts of the New Testament. For example, the Jewish concept of uncleanness came up often when Jesus was healing someone, and Mary had to be purified forty days after the birth of her son in accordance with one of the laws (chapter 12).

Similarly, the laws pertaining to sacrifice fill the first quarter of Leviticus. Without understanding the role of sacrifice for the Jews, it would be hard to understand the meaning of Christ's death (as the Letter to the Hebrews teaches), or the idea of the Eucharist as a sacrifice.

There are two major divisions in Leviticus. The first sixteen chapters tell priests how to conduct themselves, including laws of sacrifice and laws of proper foods and states of purity. Chapters 17-27 deal with the wider community and public worship.

Chapters 1-7 give us the laws of sacrifice: the holocaust (the animal that is burned on the Temple's altar), the grain offering, the peace offering, the sin offering, and the guilt offering. Jews today cannot perform these sacrifices because the Temple in Jerusalem was destroyed by the Romans in 70 A.D. Nevertheless, these laws remain important for Jews.

Chapters 8-10 tell us about the installation of Aaron and his sons and their first sacrifices. The sacrifices must be done with great precision and that point is hammered home when two of Aaron's sons are struck dead because they handled incense improperly.

Then we get to the laws regarding legal purity in chapters 11-15: clean and unclean food, the uncleanness of childbirth and the mother's purification, and two chapters about leprosy. We can see why Jesus told the lepers he cured to show themselves to the priests.

Chapter 15 is about personal uncleanness. Reading verses 25-27, we can understand the plight of the woman who suffered hemorrhages for twelve years whom Jesus healed (Mt 9:20-22; Mk 5:25-34; Lk 8:43-48).

More laws from the Book of Leviticus

Chapter 16 gives regulations for the Day of Atonement, or Yom Kippur.

Chapter 17 is the beginning of the "Code of Legal Holiness." It begins by emphasizing the sacredness of blood. Since blood was considered the seat and sign of life, even the butchering of animals was seen as having a sacrificial character.

Verse 11 tells us that "it is the blood, as the seat of life, that makes atonement." The Letter to the Hebrews in the New Testament applied that idea to the death of Christ, inasmuch as "without the shedding of blood there is no forgiveness" (Heb 9:22).

Chapter 18 is about the sanctity of sex. Marriage, as well as casual intercourse, is forbidden between men and women of various degrees of relationship. I might note that "you shall not have intercourse with your brother's wife" (verse 16) is the commandment John the Baptist accused Herod Antipas of having done. (An exception to that law is made in Deuteronomy 25:5 when a man dies and his brother is advised to marry his widow to raise up children in his name.)

Apparently some of the things condemned in this chapter were practiced by the Canaanites because the Israelites are warned not to conform to their customs.

Chapter 19 has a variety of rules of conduct, especially concerned with defending the rights of the weak. It includes the commandment, "You shall love your neighbor as yourself" (verse 18). It also commands, "Do not tattoo yourselves" (verse 28), forbids consulting fortune-tellers (verse 31), and says, "You shall treat the alien who resides with you no differently than the native born among you; have the same love for him as for yourself" (verse 34), one of numerous times that this commandment appears in the Old Testament.

Chapter 20 repeats some of the commandments but adds penalties to each, some severe, especially regarding idolatry and incest.

Chapters 21-25 deal with priestly matters and public worship. They begin with the sanctity of the priesthood, with special rules for priests governing marriage, deformities and uncleanness. For example, "The priest shall marry a virgin. Not a widow or a woman who has been divorced or a woman who has lost her honor as a prostitute, but a virgin" (21:13-14).

Priests also may not be blind, lame, have a crippled foot, be humpbacked, or afflicted with eczema, ringworm or hernia (21:18-19).

Chapter 23 has rules for the Jewish holy days, beginning with the Sabbath and then Passover, Pentecost (fifty days after Passover), New Year's Day, the Day of Atonement, and the Feast of Booths. Booths celebrated the fruit harvest. For seven days the Israelites camped in booths of branches on the roofs of their houses in commemoration of their wandering in the desert, where they dwelt in booths.

Chapter 25 concerns the sabbatical year, every seventh year when no planting is done, and the jubilee year, every fifty years when property and debts return to their original owners. However, there's no evidence that the Jews actually observed them.

4

THE BOOK OF NUMBERS

The Book of Numbers, the fourth book in the Old Testament, is a combination of history and laws. Historically, it tells the story of the 38 year journey of the Israelites from Mount Sinai to the east side of the Jordan River, ready to cross into the Promised Land. The laws relate to their experiences and need to keep order.

The book derives its name from two censuses, one taken near the start and the other near the end of the journey. They were for military purposes, so they included only the men twenty years of age or older, and did not include the Levites since they were priests. The first census found 603,550 men and the second 601,730.

The first nine chapters tell of the preparations for departure from Sinai after being there for two years and entering into a covenant with God. Interspersed among the preparations are laws, such as the ordeal for a suspected adulteress in chapter 5 and laws concerning nazarites (those who dedicate themselves to God) in chapter 6. That chapter ends with the priestly blessing, which the Catholic Church reads in the first reading at Masses on New Year's Day.

The actual journey begins with chapter 10. But this is no ordinary trip. It's a military campaign that won't end until the

Israelites conquer the tribes in Canaan. At least, that's the idea. However, this vast army is also marching with women and children and it's marching through a desert. So it's not long before the people are rebelling – in chapter 11. Even Moses' brother and sister, Aaron and Miriam, oppose him, in chapter 12, and God punishes Miriam by turning her into a leper – temporarily.

While camped in the desert of Paran, on the northeast side of the Sinai Peninsula, Moses sent twelve scouts to reconnoiter the land of Canaan. They returned and reported that the land "does indeed flow with milk and honey," but the people were fierce giants and the towns fortified. Only Caleb and Joshua thought that they could defeat them.

The others spread the word through the camp and the people were again ready to revolt. God again threatened to destroy them and again Moses spoke in their defense. God then decreed that, of all the men twenty years or more registered in the census, only Joshua and Caleb would enter the Promised Land. All the others would wander in the desert until their death.

Chapters 16 and 17 tell about the rebellion of a man named Korah and another by Dathan and Abiram. God destroyed Korah and two hundred fifty followers by fire and Dathan and Abiram and their followers were killed by being swallowed alive by an earthquake.

Chapters 18 has laws pertaining to the priests in the tribe of the Levites, their share in the food offered to God in sacrifice, the tithes due to the Levites and what they are to do with them.

Chapter 19 tells how the Israelites were to purify themselves if they touch a dead body.

The Israelites arrive east of the Jordan

Chapter 20 begins with the death of Miriam, Moses' sister, and ends with the death of Aaron, his brother. In between we have the incident at Kadesh where the Israelites again complained about the lack of water. God told Moses to order a rock to yield its water. Instead, Moses struck the rock twice with his staff, and water gushed out. Because God deemed that Moses did not have sufficient faith to work the miracle with only one blow, he told him that he would not lead the Israelite community into the Promised Land.

Chapter 21 includes the story of the bronze serpent. Again the people complained because there was no food or water. This time, as punishment, God sent serpents to bite the people, and many died. When Moses prayed to God, God told him to make a seraph and mount it on a pole. If anyone was bitten and looked at the seraph, he would be healed.

In the New Testament, Jesus referred to this incident when he told Nicodemus, "As Moses lifted up the serpent in the desert, even so must the Son of Man be lifted up, that those who believe in him may not perish, but may have life everlasting" (Jn 3:14-15).

Chapter 21 also tells of the military victories over Sihon, king of the Amorites, and the giant Og, king of Bashan, who refused to let the Israelites pass through their territories. The Israelites slaughtered all the people – men, women and children – and took possession of their lands, including sixty cities in Bashan. These victories are repeated in the Book of Deuteronomy.

The Israelites finally arrived on the plains of Moab, north-east of the Dead Sea in modern Jordan. They remained there until they crossed the Jordan River into Canaan.

Balaam and his talking ass

Chapters 22-24 might be the most fascinating part of the Book of Numbers because they tell the story of Balaam, a mysterious prophet from Mesopotamia. Balak, king of Moab, summoned Balaam to curse the Israelites. We have the story of Balaam's talking ass that balked at moving ahead because it, but not Balaam, saw an angel with a drawn sword.

Eventually, Balaam proclaimed four oracles, but instead of cursing the Israelites he blessed them, and then went his way. (However, in chapter 31, the Israelites executed Balaam when they killed five Midianite kings.)

Chapter 25 tells us that the Israelites "degraded themselves by having illicit relations with the Moabite women" (verse 1) and offered sacrifices to their god, the Baal of Peor. God told Moses to hold a public execution of those who were guilty, and 24,000 were killed. God praised Phinehas for his zeal in carrying out the execution.

The concluding chapters of Numbers include the defeat of the Midianites, the second census, and the allotment of the lands of Canaan to the various tribes after they conquered them. It was agreed that the tribes of Gad and Reuben could stay east of the Jordan, in Gilead, as long as their men aided in the conquest.

5

THE BOOK OF DEUTERONOMY

Chapter 22 of the Second Book of Kings reports that, in 622 B.C., the high priest Hilkiah found "the book of the law" in the Temple. He gave it to the scribe Shaphan who read it to King Josiah. The king then commanded the Israelites to observe the ordinances in that book, which they clearly had not been doing.

That book had to have been the Book of Deuteronomy, the fifth book in the Old Testament and the Jewish Torah. "Deuteronomy" means "second law" and much of it contains dire warnings of what would happen if the Israelites didn't follow the laws proclaimed on Mount Sinai, as we saw when we studied the Books of Exodus and Leviticus.

Deuteronomy is presented as a lengthy farewell sermon by Moses in the plains of Moab as the Israelites were preparing to cross the Jordan River into Canaan. That would have been about 1250 B.C., but the book actually was written about one hundred years before Josiah's reign.

By the time of Jesus, Deuteronomy and Psalms were probably the most important books for the Jews and the early Christians. During Jesus' temptation in the desert, Matthew's Gospel (4:1-11) has Jesus resisting the devil's three temptations by quoting three passages from Deuteronomy (8:3, 6:16 and 6:13).

Also, when Jesus is asked which commandment in the law is the greatest (Mt 22:36, Mk 12:28), he quotes Deuteronomy: "Hear, O Israel! The Lord is our God, the Lord alone! Therefore, you shall love the Lord, your God, with all your heart, and with all your soul, and with all your strength" (6:4). This remains today the daily prayer and confession of faith of observant Jews.

In his farewell sermon, Moses began with a historical review, from the time the Israelites left Mount Horeb (it's called Horeb rather than Sinai in this book). He repeated the accounts of the defeats of Sihon and the giant Og and the allotment of conquered lands that we saw in the Book of Numbers.

In chapter 5 he began to proclaim the ordinances, statutes and decrees that were part of the covenant with God, beginning with the Ten Commandments. You will notice a few differences between the Commandments listed here and those in chapter 20 of Exodus, mainly in listing "You shall not covet your neighbor's wife" as a separate Commandment, as the Catholic Church does. Exodus included the neighbor's wife with his house, slave, ox or ass.

I invite you to read, or at least skim, the laws in this book because many of them come up in later books or in the New Testament. The marriage laws in chapter 24 are interesting, and levirate marriage is prescribed in chapter 25. One has to wonder, though, how often the situation described in 25:11-12 occurred among the Israelites.

Moses' final words included curses and blessings. He commissioned Joshua to lead the Israelites into the Promised Land and blessed the twelve tribes. Then he climbed Mount Nebo, where he died and was buried at age 120.

6

THE BOOK OF JOSHUA

After God first promised Abraham that he would be the father of a great nation, his descendants the Israelites finally entered the Promised Land in the Book of Joshua – roughly 700 years later.

Between those events, Abraham's grandson Jacob (called Israel) took his family to Egypt where their descendants stayed for 430 years; Moses led the Israelites, who had grown to 600,000 men plus women and children, out of Egypt and into the desert; and God formed a covenant with these people and laid down strict laws, but allowed them to stay in the desert for forty years.

Now, according to the Book of Joshua, God gave the Israelites the land he promised them by conquering the tribes that were living there. Joshua led the people in the battles that defeated 31 kings, but the book makes it clear that it was really God who won those victories, usually miraculously. He kept the promise he first made to Abraham 700 years earlier.

We are not reading a history book here. As *The Catholic Study Bible* says, "The events that led up to Israelite possession of the land of Canaan were far more complicated than is indicated in the version of the conquest found in the Book of Joshua." Furthermore, no archaeological evidence backs up the stories in this book.

Keeping this in mind, let's see what the Book of Joshua says:

After Moses' death, God instructed Joshua to prepare for the invasion of Canaan. First Joshua sent two spies to Jericho where they went into the house of a harlot named Rahab to spend the night. When the authorities learned that they were there, Rahab hid them on the roof of the house, which had been built into the city wall. When it was dark, she let them down with a rope and the men got away.

They promised that they would save her and her family when the Israelites destroyed Jericho, and they did. Rahab married Salmon of the tribe of Judah and became the great-great-grandmother of King David. Matthew's Gospel includes Rahab in Jesus' genealogy (1:5).

So the Israelites crossed the Jordan River and the miracles began. When the priests carrying the Ark of the Covenant waded into the river, the waters parted just as they did forty years earlier at the Red Sea. The whole community marched into Canaan on dry land and camped at Gilgal, just east of Jericho.

Before conquering Jericho, though, God ordered Joshua to have all the men circumcised. We learn for the first time that "none of those born in the desert during the journey after the departure from Egypt were circumcised" (5:5). Why wait until now to have it done? We're not told.

We are told, though, that the Israelites celebrated the feast of Passover while they were camped at Gilgal. They ate of the produce of the land on the west side of the Jordan River and the manna they had eaten for 40 years ceased.

The Israelites conquer Canaan

Now they were ready for their military campaigns.

The miraculous conquest of the country of Canaan by the Israelites is told in chapters 6-12. When the conquest was finished, chapter 12 lists 31 kings who were defeated and whose lands were supposedly apportioned to the tribes of Israel.

The conquest began with Jericho. Here God had the people march around the city for six days, with seven priests blowing rams' horns. The Ark of the Covenant, signifying God's presence, was carried. On the seventh day they marched around the city seven times. Then, when the priests blew their horns, the people shouted and the walls collapsed. The people stormed the city and slaughtered all living creatures, except for the harlot Rahab, who had saved the Israelites' spies, and her family.

I have led a number of pilgrimages to the Holy Land. When we visit the modern day of Jericho the people invariably are disappointed to learn that there is no archaeological evidence of any walls that might have collapsed. Rather, archaeologists tell us that Jericho was in ruins at the time of Joshua.

After the defeat of Jericho, the Book of Joshua says that the Israelites tried to defeat the city of Ai, but could not do so at first because one of the Israelite soldiers, named Achan, had taken some of the loot from Jericho, which was forbidden. Once this was discovered, Achan was stoned to death. Then chapter 8 tells about the defeat of Ai and the slaughter of its people.

By this time, according to the book, the Hittites, Amorites, Canaanites, Perizzites, Hivites and Jebusites decided it was time to form an alliance against Israel. The Gibeonites, though, deceived Joshua by going to him dressed in shabby clothing and claiming to be from a far-off land. Joshua agreed to spare them and made an alliance with them. When their deception was discovered, Joshua kept his agreement but made the Gibeonites vassals.

Then Adonizedek, king of Jerusalem, and four other kings, learning that the Gibeonites had made peace with Israel, attacked Gibeon. Joshua came to the Gibeonites' rescue and slaughtered many of the enemy. God himself hurled great stones from the sky and "more died from these hailstones than the Israelites slew with the sword" (10:11). The five kings hid in a cave, but they were discovered and Joshua killed them.

The Israelites conquered southern Canaan and then moved up to northern Canaan. Each time God delivered the tribes into Joshua's hands and each time he killed their kings. "Thus Joshua captured the whole country, just as the Lord had foretold to Moses" (11:23).

Chapters 13 through 22 describe the distribution of the land among the Israelite tribes.

Chapters 23 and 24 report that, many years later, Joshua gathered all the tribes together at Shechem, where he lived. He recounted all that God had done for them from the time of Abraham up to that day and he urged the people to renew their covenant with the Lord, which they did. He then died at age 110.

7

THE BOOK OF JUDGES

The ending of the Book of Joshua, which we discussed in the previous chapter, gave the impression that the Israelites conquered Canaan when they defeated 31 kings. The Book of Judges quickly corrects that impression. The Israelites not only didn't destroy the Philistines, Canaanites, Hittites, Amorites, Perizzites, Hivites, and Jebusites, they lived among them, intermarried with them, and served their gods.

This angered God, the book says. Since they were not true to their covenant with God, God punished them by sending oppressors. When they repented and turned back to the true God, he sent a deliverer, a judge, to rescue them. The judge secured peace during his or her lifetime, but then the people returned to idolatry. The cycle continued over and over.

Obviously, the Israelite "judges" were really military leaders who, through their heroic deeds, rescued the people from persecution. Twelve of them appeared at various times, six "minor" judges who were apparently actually judicial officials, and six "major" judges, famous for their military exploits.

The Book of Judges tells their basically unrelated stories. The stories illustrate the Israelite theology that sin brings punishment, repentance brings deliverance. But some of the stories also include crude humor and guile on the part of the judges.

Othniel is the first judge mentioned. We're told that the people sinned enough that God allowed them to fall into the power of Cushan-rishathaim, king of Aram, for eight years. The people repented, Othniel defeated Cushan-rishathaim, and there was peace for forty years.

Then the Israelites offended God again and he allowed Eglon, king of Moab, to defeat Israel and rule them for eighteen years. This time it was Ehud who came to the rescue. He managed to get a private audience with King Eglon during which he killed him by thrusting a foot-long dagger into his belly. Eglon was so fat that the hilt went in, too, and disappeared in the fat.

Ehud left, but Eglon's attendants didn't find the king until later because they thought he was just taking a long time in the bathroom ("easing himself in the cool chamber"). Ehud made his escape and the Israelites attacked the Moabites, slaying ten thousand of them. The country had rest for eighty years.

Women to the rescue

The next time the Israelites offended the Lord, he allowed them to fall into the hands of the Canaanite king Jabin, who oppressed the Israelites for twenty years. This time it was women who came to the rescue.

Deborah was both a judge and a prophet. She organized the Israelites to defeat a Canaanite army commanded by Sisera, who was killed by another woman, Jael, to the humiliation of the Israelite commander, Barak. Sisera escaped when the Israelites defeated his army and made it to Jael's tent. While he slept, she drove a tent peg through his temple.

In the canticle of Deborah, sung after the victory, she referred to Jael as "blessed among women" (5:24). The Gospel of Luke uses that expression when Elizabeth greets Mary at the Visitation (Lk 1:42).

After Deborah defeated the army of Sisera, Israel was at peace for forty years. Then, the Book of Judges says, the Israelites again offended the Lord, who delivered them into the hands of the Midianites for seven years. This time it was Gideon who came to the rescue and his story is told in chapters 6-8.

Again there was peace for forty years, until Gideon died. And again, after his death, the Israelites abandoned themselves to the god Baal.

The murder of Gideon's sons

Gideon had seventy sons because he had many wives. They lived in Ophrah. He also had a concubine who lived in Shechem. She bore him a son named Abimelech. After Gideon died, Abimelech went to Shechem and convinced them that he, rather than Gideon's other sons, should rule them. He then went to Ophrah and killed all seventy of his brothers except the youngest, Jotham, who was hidden.

Abimelech ruled over Shechem for three years before God roused its citizens to rebel against him. Chapter 9 tells of the battle, which Abimelech won. But then he tried to conquer a neighboring city where a woman fractured his skull by dropping a millstone on him from a tower. Rather than be killed by a woman, Abimelech asked his armor-bearer to kill him with his sword.

It seems that the Israelites never learned. Again they abandoned the true God and worshipped the gods of Sidon, Moab, the Ammonites and the Philistines. So God allowed them to be oppressed for eighteen years before they acknowledged their sins and asked for God's mercy.

This time it was Jephthah who led the Israelites against the Ammonites, as told in chapter 11. Before the battle, he made a vow to the Lord that, if he returned in triumph, he would offer as a sacrifice to the Lord whoever came out of the doors of his house to meet him. When he returned, it was his daughter who was the first to do so.

Improbably, Jephthah's daughter agreed that her father had made a vow. She asked only that she be spared for two months while she "mourned her virginity." Then Jephthah killed her. And where, I've always asked myself, was her mother while this was going on?

Samson and Delilah

Five minor judges are mentioned before we get the lengthy story of Samson, told in chapters 13-16. He is listed as a judge of Israel, but his exploits are purely personal.

Samson is a tragic figure, endowed with great strength but lacking in wisdom, as his affair with Delilah showed. The announcement of his conception, by an angel to his mother, is echoed in Luke's narrative of the announcement of the conception of John the Baptist, by an angel to his father. Both men are born to a woman who had been sterile and both men take a Nazarite vow to abstain from wine and strong drink, although Samson doesn't keep that vow.

Samson also seems to prefigure Solomon to some extent. Both men became involved with foreign women and that became their downfall.

8

THE BOOK OF RUTH

The Book of Ruth is a delightful short story (only four chapters) that has long been a favorite among both Jews and Christians. It's placed in the Old Testament after the Book of Judges because the events happened during the time of the Israelite judges.

It's of particular interest to Christians because Ruth is included in the genealogy of Jesus (Mt 1:5). She was the great-grandmother of King David. I encourage you to read the book, but here's a synopsis.

The story begins in Bethlehem, where a man named Elimelech lived with his wife Naomi and their sons Mahlon and Chilion. A famine caused them to move to Moab, located to the east of the Dead Sea (in modern Jordan). The sons married Moabite women, Orpah and Ruth. But Elimelech and both sons died.

Learning that the famine in Bethlehem had ended, Naomi decided to return there. Realizing how difficult life would be for a widow without sons, she told her two daughters-in-law to remain in Moab and find other husbands, and Orpah did.

But Ruth refused, telling Naomi, "Do not ask me to abandon or forsake you! For wherever you go I will go, wherever you lodge I will lodge, your people shall be my people, and your God my God" (1:16). So Naomi and Ruth returned to Bethlehem.

In Bethlehem a man named Boaz, prominent in the community and a member of Elimelech's clan, owned barley and wheat fields. According to Jewish laws (see Lv 19:9 and Dt 24:19-23), when grains were harvested the poor, widows, aliens and orphans were permitted to glean what was not collected. Ruth, therefore, began to glean a field owned by Boaz.

Boaz noticed Ruth and learned about her faithfulness to Naomi. He told her, "May the Lord reward what you have done!" (2:12), provided her with food and water, and made sure that her gleaning was successful.

Ruth reported this to Naomi, who immediately realized that Boaz was a relative. She also knew the Jewish law that required a near relative of the same clan to marry the widow of a relative who had died without male offspring (Dt 25:5-10). So Naomi had a plan.

She learned that Boaz was going to be sleeping that night on the threshing floor. She instructed Ruth to wait until Boaz was asleep and then to lie down by his feet. She did so. In the middle of the night, Boaz awakened to find a woman at his feet.

When he asked who she was, Ruth identified herself and asked him to "spread the corner of your cloak over me, for you are my next of kin" (3:10), thus asking him to do his duty and marry her. Boaz told her that she had another relative closer to her.

Boaz then met with that closer relative and told him that Naomi was going to sell a piece of land that belonged to Elimelech. If the relative wanted to claim it, he would also have to take Ruth as his wife. The relative relinquished his claim to Boaz, who married Ruth.

9

THE FIRST BOOK OF SAMUEL

The two Books of Samuel tell the stories of three of the greatest figures in Israel's history: Samuel, Saul and David. They are a combination of sagas, in which God intervenes in their lives, and actual history. The history stretches from the last of Israel's judges, Samuel, through the establishment of Israel's monarchy and David's royal dynasty.

The First Book begins with Samuel's birth to Hannah, a barren woman who prayed for a child in the shrine at Shiloh. When Hannah bears a son, she recites a hymn that readers will recognize as having several points of resemblance with the Blessed Virgin's Magnificat of the Gospel According to Luke.

Samuel grew up in the service of the priest Eli, who had two sons, Hophni and Phinehas. But they were wicked, among other things "having relations with the women serving at the entry of the meeting tent" (1 S 2:22). One night God appeared to Samuel and told him that he would punish Eli's family.

That happened when Hophni and Phinehas took the Ark of the Covenant into battle against the Philistines. The Philistines defeated the Israelites and captured the Ark. When this was reported to Eli, then 98, he fell backward from his chair and died of a broken neck.

While the Ark was in the possession of the Philistines, they had nothing but trouble, the people being afflicted with hemorrhoids and their cities being overrun by mice. They therefore returned the Ark along with a guilt offering.

As Samuel began to judge Israel as Eli's successor, he demanded that the Israelites put away their foreign gods and worship the Lord alone. He then led an army against the Philistines and defeated them. Afterward, he continued to judge Israel.

Chapter 8 begins the establishment of the monarchy. Readers should be aware, though, that the book gives two, and sometimes three, viewpoints on most of the events, including the appointment of Saul as king, the reasons for his downfall, his relationship with David, and the circumstances of his death.

Samuel anoints Saul as king

When the people came to him asking for a king to rule over them like other nations had, Samuel was displeased because he considered the Lord to be their ruler. But he finally acquiesced to their request and anointed Saul as king. Saul is described as a handsome young man who stood head and shoulders above the people.

About a month after Saul was chosen, the Ammonites threatened a portion of Israel. The people went to Saul, who invaded the Ammonite camp with his troops and slaughtered them. After that Saul was accepted as king and his kingdom was inaugurated at Gilgal.

Chapter 12 brings the era of Israel's judges to an end with an address by Samuel. He tells the people that he has acceded to their demand for a king, but they must still obey the Lord or God will deal with them severely.

After Samuel anointed Saul king of Israel, the book moves on to the reasons why God rejected him – basically because of his disobedience to God's will as relayed by Samuel. We Christians will consider it strange that Saul's most serious disobedience occurred after his defeat of the Amalekites. Samuel told Saul that God commanded him to destroy all the men, women, children and animals of the Amalekites, but he spared Agag, their king, and kept the best of their sheep and oxen. A footnote in Catholic Bibles explains that "the interpretation of God's will attributed to Samuel is in keeping with the abhorrent practices of blood revenge prevalent among pastoral, semi-nomadic peoples such as the Hebrews had recently been. The slaughter of the innocent has never been in conformity with the will of God."

Nevertheless, that's the reason given for God's rejection of Saul. Samuel told Saul that the Lord had torn the kingdom of Israel from him and then Samuel personally killed Agag.

The anointing of David

The Lord then led Samuel to Bethlehem, to the house of Jesse, to find Saul's successor. As seven of Jesse's sons were presented, Samuel realized that God had rejected all of them. But the youngest was out tending the sheep. When he was brought in, God told Samuel that he was the one chosen. So Samuel anointed David.

Of course, Saul didn't know that. Tormented by an evil spirit, he ordered his servants to find a skillful harpist to play for him. Knowing that David was skilled as a harpist, the servants brought him to Saul. Thus David went into Saul's service, as a harpist and Saul's armor-bearer.

Chapter 17 gives us the story of David's killing the six-feet-six-inch giant Philistine, Goliath. The story is a masterpiece of storytelling, but it has no connection with the preceding events. We are reintroduced to Jesse and his family. Jesse sent David to his brothers who were fighting in Saul's army. He arrived at Saul's camp to learn that Goliath had challenged the Israelites to send a man to fight him.

David, inspired by God, told Saul that he would fight Goliath. Then we have the classic "underdog story" as David defeated the giant and cut off his head. The story shows David's character, his faith in God, and his courage – qualities necessary for the king of Israel.

David continued in Saul's service, successfully carrying out every mission Saul gave him. Saul's son Jonathan became his best friend.

When the army returned after its military victories, the women welcomed it with tambourines and dancing. They sang, "Saul has slain his thousands, and David his ten thousands." This angered Saul and from then on he tried to kill David.

Saul's attempts to kill his rival David

King Saul's jealousy of David, his attempts to kill him, and David's escapes fill 10 chapters in the First Book of Samuel, beginning with the middle of chapter 18. David does nothing without first consulting the Lord.

The first attempt on David's life was in Saul's home, where David was playing the harp as at other times. Suddenly Saul threw his spear at David, hoping to nail him to the wall, but David escaped.

Saul then thought he could get the Philistines to kill David. He told David that he would give him his daughter Michal in marriage if he brought him the foreskins of 100 Philistines. David and his men slew 200 Philistines and David counted out their foreskins before the king (as distasteful as that is). So David married Michal.

Saul planned to kill David the following day, but that night Michal let David down through a window and he escaped. Jonathan, Saul's son, also helped David even after Saul told him that Jonathan would never succeed him as king as long as David lived.

David went to Ahimelech, the priest in the city of Nob, and asked for bread for his men, lying that he was on a mission for the king. Ahimelech gave him bread that had been offered as a sacrifice and also Goliath's sword. When Saul learned about that he sent his men to kill all the men, women, children and animals of the city of Nob.

David was then a fugitive. He took his parents to Moab for their protection and they remained there while David was on the run. David, though, went back to Judah.

Twice, while Saul and his men were chasing David and his men, David had the opportunity to kill Saul, but he did not because Saul was God's anointed one and David respected that. The first time was when Saul went into a cave "to ease nature" (24:4). David sneaked up and cut off the end of Saul's mantle.

The second time was at night, when David entered Saul's

camp while everyone was sleeping and took Saul's spear and water jug. After both episodes, Saul admitted his guilt and promised not to harm David.

In between those episodes is the story of Nabal and Abigail (chapter 25). David sent servants to Nabal, asking for provisions for his people, but Nabal refused. This angered David and he and four hundred men started down to wipe out Nabal's family. But Nabal's servants told Abigail what had happened and she loaded up asses filled with provisions.

Meeting David, Abigail prostrated herself and begged for his mercy. David accepted the provisions and sent her back home. When she told Nabal what had happened, "he became like a stone" (25:37) and ten days later God struck him and he died.

David then sent a proposal of marriage to Abigail, and she accepted. David also married Ahinoam. Meanwhile, Saul gave David's first wife, Michal, Saul's daughter, to another man, a man called Palti.

The death of Israel's first king

At the end of chapter 26 of the First Book of Samuel, King Saul promised not to try to harm David again. David, however, didn't trust Saul, so he did something we wouldn't expect: He and his six hundred men joined forces with the hated Philistines! Specifically, with King Achish of Gath.

He and his men lived in Ziklag for sixteen months. They made raids on the Geshurites, Girzites and Amalekites, but David told Achish that they were raiding the Israelites. They didn't leave a man or woman alive who could tell Achish what they really did. So Achish trusted David, thinking to himself that David's people must really detest him.

Then the Philistines mustered to fight against Saul, and David and his men went with Achish, seemingly intending to fight against the Israelites.

The story then shifts to Saul, who was dismayed by the force against him. He consulted a witch, asking her to conjure up the ghost of Samuel, who had died. She did so and Samuel told Saul that he and his sons would be killed in the coming battle and his kingdom would be given to David.

What about this conjuring up a ghost? The footnote here says that God may permit a departed soul to appear to the living and disclose things unknown to them. But the apparition would have been due, not to the summons of the witch, but to God's will.

The story again shifts back to David. As he and his men tried to join the Philistines, their lords asked Achish who those Hebrews were. Achish vouched for them, but the Philistine chiefs weren't convinced and demanded that Achish send them back. He did.

When they got back to Ziklag, though, they discovered that Amalekites had overrun the city, set it on fire, and taken their wives and children captive, including David's wives Ahinoam and Abigail. David and his men chased the Amalekites, killed them all and rescued their wives and children. David brought back all the booty the Amalekites had taken and sent gifts to the elders of Judah.

Back to Saul. The battle against the Philistines ended as Samuel told Saul it would. Saul's sons were killed and Saul was wounded. He asked his armor-bearer to finish him off, but he refused to do so. Therefore, Saul took his own sword and fell upon it. When the Philistines found his body, they cut off his head.

Three days after Saul's death, David was at Ziklag when a runner appeared from Saul's camp. He said that he was an Amalekite who had been in the battle. He said that he came across Saul, badly wounded, and Saul asked him to finish him off. Therefore, he said, he did so, and he brought Saul's crown and armlet to David.

If the Amalekite expected to be rewarded, he was badly mistaken. David had him killed because he had dared to desecrate the Lord's anointed. David then recited a heroic elegy for Israel's first king and his son Jonathan.

10

THE SECOND BOOK OF SAMUEL

The Second Book of Samuel gives us a theological interpretation of the reign of David, Israel's greatest king. It emphasizes the point that the man who conquered Jerusalem and made it Israel's religious center had to have been chosen by God himself.

After the death of Saul, David became king of Judah, in Hebron, while Saul's son Ishbaal ruled the northern kingdom of Israel. There followed a 7½ year war between the house of David and the house of Saul, which ended with the death of Ishbaal while he was asleep in his bedroom. The authors make it clear, though, that David was innocent of Ishbaal's death, and he put to death those who murdered him.

God was good to David while he was king of Judah in Hebron. The beginning of chapter 3 lists the names of his six sons born there, by six different wives.

After Ishbaal's death, the elders of Israel asked David to become their king. He ruled the combined kingdoms for thirty-three years.

His first move was to conquer Jerusalem, still inhabited by the Jebusites. He built his palace there and took more concubines and wives. Eleven more children were born there.

David then decided it was time to bring the Ark of the Covenant into Jerusalem. Ever since it was returned by the Philistines, it had been in the house of Abinadab. The Ark symbolized the presence of the Lord and, therefore, could be handled only by those who were consecrated.

As it was being carried, a man named Uzza tried to keep it from tipping. When he touched it, God became angry and killed him. This is pretty harsh, obviously, but it demonstrated the holiness of the Ark.

David left the Ark in the house of a Gittite for three months, and then tried again. As the procession brought it into Jerusalem, David danced and leapt before it, clad only in a linen apron. His wife Michal, whom he reclaimed after Saul's death, watched him.

When they were alone, she rebuked him for exposing himself to the slave girls. David replied that he was dancing for the Lord and, although he might be lowly in Michal's esteem, he would be honored by the slave girls. The authors add that Michal remained childless to the day of her death.

We now come to chapter 7, one of the most important parts of the Old Testament. Having brought the Ark into Jerusalem, David thought he should build a temple for it. However, the Lord told the prophet Nathan to tell David that the Lord did not want a temple. Rather, the Lord, who had been with David wherever he went, would not only make David famous but would establish a dynasty after him that would last forever.

This is the basis for messianic expectation after the destruction of Jerusalem in 586 B.C., and what the archangel Gabriel alluded to when he appeared to Mary and told her that God would give her son Jesus "the throne of David his father" (Lk 1:32).

The story of David and Bathsheba

The Old Testament is not afraid to detail the human failings of the man chosen by God to be Israel's greatest king. However, it also tells us of David's repentance and God's punishment for his sins.

Chapters 11 and 12 of the Second Book of Samuel give us the familiar story of David and Bathsheba. An idle king saw a beautiful woman bathing and, using his kingly power, sent men to take her to the palace, where he had sex with her, knowing full well that she was married to Uriah the Hittite. We are told nothing about Bathsheba's feelings about the affair, but apparently she didn't resist.

Bathsheba became pregnant and let David know. David tried to make it appear that the child was Uriah's by making it possible for him to sleep with his wife. Failing that, he ordered his general, Joab, to make sure that Uriah was killed in battle. Then David took Bathsheba as his wife. The last sentence in chapter 11 is, "But the Lord was displeased with what David had done."

So God sent the prophet Nathan to indict David for his sins. He told David that the sword would never depart from his house, that his sons would rebel against him, and that one of them would lie with his wives in broad daylight.

David repented and God accepted the repentance. However, as punishment to David, he said that Bathsheba's son would die. David tried to change the Lord's mind through fasting and other penances, but the punishment remained. Afterward, David comforted Bathsheba and she bore another son, Solomon, who would succeed David as king.

The stories that follow show how Nathan's prophecy that

the sword would not depart from David's house was fulfilled. First, in chapter 13, is the rape of David's daughter Tamar by Amnon, David's oldest son. The narrator of the story goes into detail about the lust that Amnon felt for Tamar, how he lured her into his bedroom, and how he raped her.

David learned of the rape and was angry, but did nothing since Amnon was his first-born. But David's son Absalom, filled with hatred for Amnon for what he did, was determined to take revenge on behalf of his sister. The opportunity came two years later and he successfully carried out his plan. Amnon is killed.

Fearing retribution, Absalom fled to Geshur, where he stayed for three years while David was torn between his mourning over Amnon's death and his longing for Absalom. Chapter 14 tells the story of a woman of Tekoa who convinced David to allow Absalom to return to Jerusalem. However, David decreed that Absalom was not to appear before him.

That continued for two years until Absalom begged to be allowed to appear before David. Finally David relented and he and Absalom were reconciled.

But not for long. Amnon's death put Absalom next in line for the throne, and he was impatient to have that throne.

Absalom's rebellion against King David

Chapters 15-19 of the Second Book of Samuel tell us how God continued to punish David for his sin with Bathsheba and the killing of Uriah, her husband. This time it's the rebellion of David's son Absalom. Absalom organized an army in Hebron and marched against Jerusalem.

When he learned that Absalom was coming, David fled

from Jerusalem with his household, except for ten concubines. As they fled, they met various people along the way (and would meet them again on their return). David made the procession a penitential rite, walking barefoot, and even allowing a man named Shimei to curse him.

The action shifts from David to Absalom, who entered Jerusalem. On the advice of a man named Ahithophel, he had sex with his father's concubines, pitching a tent on the roof so all the people could see when he visited the women.

Then Ahithophel and Hushai gave conflicting advice on how to track down and defeat David. Absalom accepted Hushai's advice (so Ahithophel hanged himself). But Hushai sent messengers to David to let him know what was going to happen. David prepared for battle. Persuaded not to accompany the troops, he gave instructions not to harm Absalom.

David's forces defeated Absalom's, and David's general, Joab, ignored David's orders to be gentle with Absalom. Absalom's mule passed under a terebinth tree and his hair became tangled in the branches. While he was hanging there, Joab killed him.

When the news reached David, he mourned for his son, going to his room and crying, "My son Absalom! My son, my son Absalom! If only I had died instead of you, Absalom, my son, my son!" (19:1). Joab had to convince him that all his men would desert him if he didn't stop turning a victory into mourning. David then returned to Jerusalem and reconciled with those he met when he was escaping from the city.

Chapter 19 ends with tension between Israel in the north and Judah in the south. That tension broke out in chapter 20 with a rebellion of the Israelites led by a man named Sheba, obviously showing dissatisfaction with David's rule.

David's general Joab again showed his ruthlessness by murdering Amasa, the man David sent to rally the Judahites. Then Joab and his brother Abashai chased down Sheba, who retreated to the town of Abel Beth-maacah.

As the troops were trying to batter down the walls, a woman asked Joab if he was trying to destroy the city. When Joab said that he only wanted Sheba, the woman convinced the people to cut off Sheba's head and throw it to Joab. End of rebellion.

Chapters 21-24 are appendices that seem to be random stories about things that happened during David's reign. They include a lengthy song of thanksgiving that David sang and his last words. There's also the story of David's punishment, actually inflicted on others, for ordering a census, considered wrong because it implied a lack of faith in the Lord.

11

THE FIRST BOOK OF KINGS

The First and Second Books of Kings contain the history of the two kingdoms of Judah and Israel for a period of 400 years, from about 961 B.C. to 561 B.C., from the death of David to the destruction of Jerusalem and the end of the monarchy.

The First Book of Kings begins with the reign of Solomon. He almost didn't become king. Before David's death, Solomon's half-brother Adonijah was proclaimed king by Joab, David's general, and some of David's other followers. But Bathsheba, Solomon's mother, and the prophet Nathan thwarted their plans by reporting the matter to David. David kept his promise to Bathsheba and saw to it that Solomon succeeded him.

After David's death, Solomon ruthlessly secured his kingdom by ordering the deaths of Adonijah, Joab and others. Of course, that takes 35 verses in chapter 2.

Then, in chapter 3, we learn about Solomon's wisdom. In the first of two times when the Lord appeared to him in a dream, Solomon asked for wisdom – an understanding heart. As an example, we hear the famous story of how he determined the true mother of a child.

For the first time, and the last, the kingdom was at peace. Solomon ruled from the Euphrates River to the Mediterranean

Sea and to the border with Egypt. We are told how prosperous Solomon was, including 12,000 chariot horses.

It was time to build the Temple, Solomon's most important accomplishment in the view of the writers. It took twenty years, using the work of 30,000 workmen, and the Bible goes into great detail to describe the Temple and its furnishings. Solomon also took thirteen years to build his palace, and again we get great detail.

The Temple was dedicated with a lengthy prayer (45 verses) by Solomon. Then the Lord appeared to Solomon in a dream a second time and promised to establish his kingdom forever if he and his descendants were faithful to him. If not, though, the Lord said that he would cut off Israel and repudiate the Temple.

Chapter 10 reports the visit of the Queen of Sheba (probably modern Yemen) and how impressed she was with Solomon's kingdom. We hear of his great wealth: "King Solomon surpassed in riches and wisdom all the kings of the earth. And the whole world sought audience with Solomon, to hear from him the wisdom which God had put in his heart" (10:23-24).

However, Solomon wasn't as wise as he thought. As part of his wealth, he had 700 wives and 300 concubines, many of them foreigners. So all of his piety, wisdom, wealth and prestige meant nothing after he intermarried with pagan wives and turned his heart to their gods.

Therefore, since Solomon had not kept the Lord's covenant and statutes, God determined to tear away his kingdom. However, for the sake of his father David, he would not do it during Solomon's lifetime, but during that of his son.

Solomon ruled Israel for forty years.

The great prophet Elijah enters history

Beginning with chapter 12 of the First Book of Kings, the Old Testament tells us what happened to Israel after King Solomon's death in 922 B.C. Specifically, the kingdom broke in two, with ten tribes forming the kingdom of Israel in the north and two tribes becoming the kingdom of Judah in the south. The two kingdoms warred against each other.

Jerusalem remained the capital of Judah. As far as the authors were concerned, Jerusalem's Temple was the only legitimate place for worship and the kings were judged according to their loyalty or disloyalty to the Lord in terms of worship there. This meant that the worship of those in Israel, where King Jeroboam established shrines in Dan and Bethel, was illegitimate.

Chapters 12 through 16 tell us about the reigns of three kings in Judah and six kings in Israel, the latter usually dying violently because of the sins they committed. This culminated with the beginning of the reign of Israel's King Ahab in 869 B.C. Ahab "did evil in the sight of the Lord more than any of his predecessors" (16:30). He married Jezebel and went over to the worship of Baal, building a temple to him in Samaria.

That's when the great prophet Elijah, one of the most important figures in the Old Testament, entered history, in chapter 17. He struggled to preserve the worship of Yahweh against Ahab and Jezebel.

First we learn that Elijah told Ahab that there would be a severe drought. He went to a place east of the Jordan River where he was fed by ravens. Then he moved to Sidon (in modern Lebanon) where he stayed with a widow and her son, miraculously providing enough flour for them to live for a year. Then, when the widow's son died, Elijah restored him to life.

With all that as an introduction to Elijah, chapter 18 tells the famous story of Elijah competing with the 450 prophets of Baal and the 400 prophets of Asherah on Mount Carmel. He challenged them to call upon Baal to send down fire to consume two bulls. After they tried all day long, Elijah had them pour jars of water over the sacrifice several times before praying to the God of Abraham, Isaac and Israel. God then sent fire down to consume the holocaust and lapped up the water in the trench.

As the people praised God, Elijah had them seize Baal's prophets. They took them to a brook where Elijah slit their throats.

When Ahab told Jezebel what Elijah had done, she vowed revenge, so Elijah fled for his life. He went first to Beer-sheba in Judah and then walked forty days and forty nights (reminiscent of the forty years the Israelites were in the desert) to Horeb (or Sinai), the mountain where God gave Moses the Ten Commandments.

The authors want us to know that it was fitting that Elijah, whose mission it was to reestablish the covenant, should return to Mount Horeb. There he experienced wind, storms, earthquakes and fire before hearing a tiny whispering sound that signified the presence of God.

God talked to him as he had done to Moses. He sent him back to Israel, thus indicating that he had not abandoned the people.

Upon his return, Elijah threw his cloak over Elisha, indicating that he would be his successor. Elisha immediately followed Elijah as his attendant, but we don't hear about him again until the Second Book of Kings.

Instead, in chapter 20, the action switches to battles between King Ahab of Israel and King Ben-hadad of Aram (modern Syria). There are many elements of Holy War in this lengthy chapter, with God promising victory not only in the mountains but also in the plain; in other words, throughout the world.

As part of a Holy War, the defeated king is expected to be put to death. When Ahab failed to do so and released Ben-hadad, an unnamed prophet (not Elijah) told Ahab that he would pay with his own life.

Elijah vs. Ahab and Jezebel

Chapter 21 gives us the story of Ahab and Naboth. When Ahab wanted to buy a vineyard that Naboth owned next to the palace, and Naboth refused, Ahab's wife Jezebel took matters into her hands. She arranged for scoundrels to accuse Naboth of cursing God and king, and Naboth was stoned to death. Then Ahab went to take possession of the vineyard.

However, he was met by Elijah, who told him that God condemned him, not only for what he and Jezebel did to Naboth, but for all the other evil they had done. Elijah told Ahab that dogs would lick his blood where they had licked up Naboth's, and dogs would devour Jezebel. Ahab repented by putting on sackcloth, so the Lord told Elijah that he would bring evil upon Ahab's house, not while Ahab lived, but during the reign of his son. Nevertheless, the predictions would remain.

Then King Jehoshaphat of Judah made a pact with King Ahab of Israel to fight against Aram. Before going into battle, they called upon their prophets to see if they would be successful. The prophets told them what they wanted to hear: they would be victorious.

So they called upon one more prophet, Micaiah, who said that the vision he saw was of the Lord wanting to deceive Ahab so he would go into battle and fall. For this prophecy, Micaiah was put into prison.

So Jehoshaphat and Ahab went into battle, Ahab disguising himself so the enemy wouldn't know that he was the king of Israel. Nevertheless, a lucky archer hit Ahab with an arrow between the joints of his breastplate. He died and his blood flowed to the bottom of his chariot, where it was licked up by dogs when it was washed.

Jezebel's death didn't occur until chapter 9 of the Second Book of Kings. Eunuchs threw her from a second floor and her body was left for dogs to devour.

12

THE SECOND BOOK OF KINGS

The Second Book of Kings begins with the death of King Ahaziah of Israel, the son of Ahab and Jezebel, in 849 B.C., and concludes in 561 B.C. after the destruction of the Kingdom of Judah. However, it also includes stories about the prophets Elijah and Elisha circulated by their disciples until they became legends. They include numerous miracles.

We met Elijah in the First Book of Kings, when he was combating Ahab and Jezebel. In the first chapter of the Second Book, he predicted the death of King Ahaziah. Then, when Ahaziah sent two companies of fifty men to bring him in, he commanded fire to come down from heaven to destroy the companies.

Chapter 2 tells about Elijah being taken up to heaven in a flaming chariot with flaming horses, in a whirlwind. Elisha, who was walking with him, picked up Elijah's mantle and inherited his spirit of prophecy.

Then there follow fourteen stories in which Elisha is involved in one way or another, some of which are strange indeed. There's the story, for example, of some small boys who jeered at Elisha, "Go up, baldhead, go up, baldhead." Elisha cursed them and two bears came out of the woods and tore 42 of the children to pieces (2:23-24). Footnotes here and in the story about Elijah calling down fire (second paragraph above) say only that the stories were told to enhance the dignity of the prophets and to reflect the power of God.

In chapter 3 we get a war story that highlights Elisha's role. He gave advice to the kings of Israel, Judah and Edom in a battle against Moab. The battle itself is strange because the Moabites saw water that they thought was blood, possibly caused by the red sandstone in a wadi. They thought that the three kings warred against themselves, so they went out to collect spoils. Then the three kings attacked and destroyed them, as Elisha had predicted.

There's the story of Elisha predicting that a Shunammite woman will bear a child. A few years after the child is born, he dies, but Elisha restores him to life.

There's another story of Elisha multiplying twenty barley loaves and some corn to feed one hundred people, with some left over.

The story of the cure of Naaman, the army commander of the king of Aram, of leprosy is read during Catholic Masses, so should be familiar. It's complex but it includes Naaman's declaration that there is no God in all the earth except in Israel, an astounding confession from a pagan.

The story of the siege of Samaria by Aram starts comically, with the king of Aram thinking that he has a traitor in his midst because Israel always knew where he was going to strike. Of course, it was Elisha who told the king of Israel. But then the story gets serious as the siege resulted in the Israelites eating their own children. Then the humor returns when an entire army fled before a few lepers who were out looking for a meal.

The fall of the Kingdom of Israel

There might be a couple of biblical experts who can keep the history of Israel and Judah straight, but it's surely impossible for most of us. From the middle of chapter 8 through chapter 17, when the Kingdom of Israel is destroyed, the Second Book of Kings tells us about the reigns of twenty kings and one queen. They reigned from 849 B.C. to 722 B.C.

To make it even more complicated, there are two kings named Joash, one in Judah and one in Israel, and there are similar names like Ahaziah, Azariah and Amaziah, to say nothing about Joash, Jehoash and Jehoahaz. I won't try to straighten them out, but do read those chapters to see what was happening during those 127 years.

This was a particularly bloody period in Israel's history. For example, Jehu, who had been anointed on orders from the prophet Elisha, killed both King Joram of Israel and King Ahaziah of Judah. Then he ordered the murder of Jezebel, who had been the wife of King Ahab, and allowed dogs to devour her body. Then he ordered the killing of all seventy of Ahab's descendants in Judah, followed by the same thing in Samaria.

Jehu, though, was considered one of the good guys because he destroyed the temple of Baal and rooted out the worship of Baal in Israel.

The one queen in this history was no better than the men. Athaliah learned that her son, Ahaziah, had been killed, so she killed off the whole royal family in Judah, except for Joash who was saved by his nurse. When Joash was seven, his supporters put him on the throne and killed Athaliah. Joash then reigned in Jerusalem for forty years.

While the kings were fighting against each other, they also had to fight against other countries, so we learn that Amaziah slew ten thousand Edomites.

There's nothing very religious in these stories except that the authors constantly let us know that the kings, especially those in Israel, "did evil in the sight of the Lord."

King Jeroboam II of Israel reigned from 786 B.C. to 746 B.C. Surprisingly, it was a time of peace and prosperity for Israel. It was also when two of the minor prophets, Amos and Hosea, arrived on the scene. Amos railed against the injustice and idolatry he found in Israel and prophesied the overthrow of the country and the captivity of the people.

Hosea, who was married to a prostitute, described the relation between God and Israel in terms of marriage and prophesied the punishment of Israel for its infidelity and idolatry.

The prophecies came true in chapter 17 when Assyria conquered Israel and deported the Israelites to Assyria. Then people from other countries settled in Israel and began to worship their gods.

This came about, the author wrote, because the Israelites sinned against the Lord and because they venerated other gods. They did not listen to the prophets and rejected the covenant that God had made with their fathers. The authors also warned Judah that the same thing could happen there.

Nebuchadnezzar conquers Jerusalem

The final days of the kingdom of Judah are recounted in chapters 18-25 of the Second Book of Kings. Judah survived for

136 years after the conquest of the kingdom of Israel in 722 B.C.

After Assyria conquered Israel, it attacked Judah in 701 B.C. Judah was ruled by King Hezekiah, who had the prophet Isaiah as a counselor. Isaiah had begun his prophesying in 742 B.C. after having a vision and the voice of the Lord saying, "Whom shall I send?" Isaiah replied, "Here I am; send me!" (Is 6:8).

Isaiah convinced Hezekiah that God would protect Jerusalem. When Sennacherib, king of Assyria, reached Jerusalem, the angel of the Lord struck down 185,000 of his men and Sennacherib returned to Nineveh, where he was slain by two of his sons.

Hezekiah was considered a good king, but his successors, Manasseh and Amon, were not: they "did evil in the sight of the Lord." Isaiah predicted that Judah would be destroyed because of Manasseh's sins.

Then came King Josiah, during whose reign we had a remarkable occurrence. While work was being done in the Temple the high priest Hilkiah found "the book of the law," obviously unknown to that generation or, presumably, many previous generations.

Josiah was so aroused by the book that he commanded that it be read in its entirety to the people and he made a covenant before the Lord that they would follow the ordinances, statutes and decrees that were written in the book.

Josiah began a thorough reform, influenced by the prophet Micah, that purged the country of pagan elements, not only in Judah but also in the former kingdom of Israel. He commanded that Passover be observed as stipulated in the book, the first time it had been so observed since the time of Joshua.

The authors said about Josiah, "Before him there had been no king who turned to the Lord as he did, with his whole heart, his whole soul, and his whole strength, in accord with the entire law of Moses; nor could any after him compare with him" (23:25).

But then Josiah was killed in a battle against Egypt and his successors went back to their old ways. The prophet Jeremiah opposed the return to idolatry and was rewarded for his opposition by arrest, imprisonment and public disgrace.

While this was going on in Judah, Babylon conquered Assyria and moved against Judah. Babylonian King Nebuchadnezzar captured Jerusalem for the first time and deported King Jehoiachin to Babylon, replacing him with Zedekiah.

From about 598 to 587 B.C., Jeremiah tried to counsel Zedekiah, urging him not to rebel against Babylon and not to make a pact with Egypt. Nevertheless, Zedekiah did rebel and King Nebuchadnezzar laid siege to Jerusalem. After nearly two years, when the people were starving, the walls were breached. Zedekiah tried to escape but was captured near Jericho.

Nebuchadnezzar then sent Nebuzaradan to Jerusalem where he burned the Temple and all the houses. He led the people into exile in Babylon.

13

THE BOOKS OF CHRONICLES

The two Books of Chronicles repeat the Jewish history from Adam to the destruction of Jerusalem – in other words, through the twelve books of the Bible I've already discussed in this book. Do we really have to repeat all that?

It appears that both Jews and Christians have never known quite what to do with Chronicles. Since the books end with the same events recounted in the Second Book of Kings, and since they serve as a sort of supplement to the books of Samuel and Kings, Christians put Chronicles after Kings and before the books of Ezra and Nehemiah. Besides, there's evidence that Chronicles, Ezra and Nehemiah once formed a single literary work.

The Hebrew Bible, though, has Chronicles at the very end, even after Ezra and Nehemiah. In that way, the Jewish scriptures end with the decree from King Cyrus of Persia that enabled the people of Judah to return to Jerusalem and rebuild their Temple. Ever since the destruction of the Second Temple in the year 70 A.D., the last words in the Hebrew Bible have been a call to return to Jerusalem.

The First Book of Chronicles begins with Adam and concludes with King David's reign. The Second Book begins with Solomon and concludes with that decree by Cyrus.

The first nine chapters of the first book are a trivia geek's delight since they consist of genealogies. If you want to know who the children of Reuben or Gad (two of Jacob's sons) were, you can learn it here. Otherwise, skip ahead to the history of David.

The Chronicler, writing about 400 B.C., included none of the negative things we learned about David, such as his adultery with Bathsheba or the two revolts by his sons. He was much more interested in emphasizing David's religious influence – in the fact that he made Jerusalem the center of the true worship of the Lord.

He continued that emphasis in the Second Book, with Solomon's great achievement of the building of the Temple. His purpose was to impress upon his readers the supreme importance of the Temple in order to convince them that their future had to include careful observance of the rituals handed down by God to David and preserved by the remnant that survived the exile in Babylon and returned to Jerusalem.

The Chronicler's history from Solomon through the destruction of Jerusalem by the Babylonians concentrated on the kingdom of Judah, with mention of the kingdom of Israel only when necessary. The Chronicler believed that the people of the northern kingdom were in schism because they did not worship in Jerusalem's Temple.

The division between Jews and Samaritans took place when the people of the northern kingdom (the Samaritans) intermarried among people the Assyrians brought into their territory. So far as the Chronicler was concerned (and the Jews at the time of Christ), the Samaritans were not true Jews.

The only true Jews, as far as the Chronicler was concerned, were those in exile in Babylon. It was time for them to return to Jerusalem.

14

THE BOOK OF ISAIAH

Christian Bibles follow the Second Book of Chronicles with the Book of Ezra, when the Jews in Babylon were permitted to return to the Holy Land. However, I'm going to write about some of the other books because they are concerned, in one way or another, with the exile in Babylon.

First of all, there were the prophets. I'm not going to try to summarize all eighteen of the prophetic books, but you should at least know how they fit into the Jewish history.

I already mentioned that Hosea and Amos prophesied in the northern kingdom of Israel (where Elijah and Elisha also spent most of their time) and that Isaiah and Micah were advisers to the kings of Judah before that kingdom fell. The prophecies of Zephaniah, Nahum and Habakkuk also date from this period.

The Book of Isaiah is considered the most valuable Old Testament book for the New Testament, and it is also the second longest book in the Bible, after the Book of Psalms. Because of its importance, I'll write about it in more detail than the other prophetic books, although I won't cover the entire book.

The book is an anthology of poems, beautifully written by the greatest of the prophets and by his disciples. It is really three books spanning three centuries up to about 500 B.C. The first 39 chapters were written by the prophet Isaiah himself, who lived in Jerusalem from about 765 B.C. until sometime after 701 B.C., although there are additions by his disciples even here. He tried to preserve the Davidic dynasty and the holy city of Jerusalem.

Chapters 40-55, known as Second Isaiah, were written near the end of the Babylonian Exile in the sixth century B.C., so this was after the destruction of Jerusalem. And chapters 56-66, Third Isaiah, were composed sometime after the exile to restore the people's hopes during a dismal time in their history.

The prophet Isaiah was born in Jerusalem and apparently trained in a school for scribes. He married a prophetess and they had at least two sons. He was an adviser to both Ahaz and Hezekiah, but neither took his advice to rely on God rather than make alliances with other countries. That's when he began to make his predictions of dire things to come to the citizens of Jerusalem.

Isaiah indicts Israel and Judah

The book begins with an indictment of Israel and Judah for being a "sinful nation, people laden with wickedness, evil race, corrupt children! They have forsaken the Lord and spurned the Holy One of Israel" (1:4).

Isaiah takes the people to task for not caring for the needy. He quotes God as saying that he has had enough of their sacrifices of lambs and goats. He will not listen to their prayers because their hands are full of blood.

Instead of all their festivals, God says, "Put away your misdeeds from before my eyes; cease doing evil; learn to do good.

Make justice your aim: redress the wronged, hear the orphan's plea, defend the widow" (1:16-17).

Because of their sins, God will take vengeance on his foes, but then, "Zion shall be redeemed by judgment, and her repentant ones by justice" (1:27). This verse is the key to the whole Book of Isaiah. After God's judgment, Zion's survivors will return to God.

Then, Isaiah says, "The mountain of the Lord's house shall be established as the highest mountain and raised above the hills. All nations shall stream toward it" (2:2). From Zion God "shall judge between the nations, and impose terms on many peoples. They shall beat their swords into plowshares and their spears into pruning hooks; one nation shall not raise the sword against another, nor shall they train for war again" (2:4).

In chapter 6 we learn about Isaiah's call to be a prophet (6:1-13). This was the vision he had during which an angel touched his mouth with a burning ember, removing his sins. When he heard God's voice saying, "Whom shall I send?", he replied, "Send me!"

"The virgin shall be with child"

Chapter 7 tells us of an incident that took place when King Pekah of the northern kingdom of Israel allied with King Rezin of Syria and attacked Judah, in chapter 16 of the Second Book of Kings. It's here that we have Isaiah's prophecy while talking with King Ahaz, "The Lord himself will give you this sign: the virgin shall be with child, and bear a son, and shall name him Immanuel" (7:14). Christians have always followed St. Matthew's Gospel in seeing the fulfillment of that prophecy in the birth of Christ to the Blessed Virgin (see Mt 1:18-25).

Isaiah didn't know the full force of his prediction, because he went on to tell Ahaz, "Before the child learns to reject the bad and choose the good, the land of those two kings whom you dread (Pekah and Rezin) shall be deserted" (7:16). However, the Holy Spirit was preparing for another Nativity which alone could fulfill the divinely given terms of Immanuel's mission.

Chapters 9:7 to 10:4 contain Isaiah's prediction of the fall of the northern kingdom of Israel. This happened in 721 B.C. when Assyria conquered the kingdom, becoming the unconscious instrument of God's wrath. (The story is in chapter 17 of the Second Book of Kings.)

Chapter 11:1-16 is the prediction of a messianic king from "the stump of Jesse" (David's father). Christians believe, of course, that that king is Christ.

Chapter 19 is a prediction of the conversion of Egypt and Assyria, when "Israel shall be a third party with Egypt and Assyria, a blessing in the midst of the land" (24).

Chapters 24-27 are what is known as the "Apocalypse of Isaiah." Apocalyptic literature uses symbols to present God's design for the world. The name means "draws aside the veil."

Compared with the apocalyptic language in Ezekiel and Daniel, Isaiah's is rather subdued, but we might look at some of it in chapter 25: "On this mountain the Lord of hosts will provide for all peoples a feast of rich food and choice wines, juicy, rich food and pure choice wines" (verse 6).

Some biblical exegetes see this as adding a model to the sacred meals of the Old Testament that became absorbed into the New Testament's theology of the Eucharist. Just as God provided manna for the Israelites in the wilderness, so the Eucharist imparts spiritual help for those who receive it.

There is also Isaiah's statement that the Lord of hosts "will destroy death forever" (25:8). Although somewhat implicit, up to this point the Old Testament seldom said much about what happens after a person dies.

An historic perspective

Chapters 28-39 are later additions to the book, giving an historic perspective from chapters 18 and 19 of the Second Book of Kings. Chapter 29 begins with, "Woe to Ariel, Ariel, the city where David encamped!" Ariel is either a poetic name for Jerusalem or an archaic name when it was a Jebusite city before David conquered it. This is a prediction that the city will come under siege. That happened when Assyria turned against Judah.

Isaiah had long counseled King Hezekiah not to ally Judah with Egypt and against Assyria. If Judah was looking for someone other than "the Holy One of Israel" for protection, Isaiah said, both the protector (Egypt) and the protected (Judah) would fall (Is 31:1-3). Hezekiah, though, didn't listen.

In the year 701 B.C., King Sennacherib of Assyria attacked Judah. His forces speedily swept through the country. Assyrian historical records list 46 cities that he captured before he surrounded Jerusalem.

Isaiah supported Hezekiah as the king refused to surrender. Hezekiah fortified the city walls and dug a trench to bring water from the Gihon spring outside the city to the pool of Siloam inside. Isaiah encouraged the people, telling them that God would preserve his city.

Isaiah predicted, "Assyria shall fall by a sword not wielded by man, no mortal sword shall devour him; he shall flee before the sword, and his young men shall be impressed as laborers. He shall rush past his crag in panic, and his princes shall flee in terror from his standard, says the Lord who has a fire in Zion and a furnace in Jerusalem" (31:8-9).

As we saw in the Second Book of Kings, the angel of the Lord struck down 185,000 men in the Assyrian camp. That figure seems highly improbable, but the Assyrians gave up the siege. Isaiah's prophecy was fulfilled.

The Second Book of Isaiah

What is known as Second Isaiah, or Deutero-Isaiah, (chapters 40-55) was written toward the end of the Babylonian Exile by an unknown prophet, about 150 years after Isaiah prophesied in Jerusalem. While Isaiah advised Judah's kings about protecting Jerusalem, this prophet knows that Jerusalem has been destroyed and looks forward to its reconstruction. He exhorts the Judahites to return to Jerusalem and begin the task of rebuilding their lives.

We can understand their reluctance to do that, so they need some prodding. They have been in Babylon for almost fifty years and they know that Jerusalem was destroyed. Most of them were born in Babylon. Besides, they believe that God has forgotten them. Why would they want to pack up and move back to that land that they consider, literally, God-forsaken?

The prophet acknowledges all that, but begs to disagree: "Zion said, 'The Lord has forsaken me; my Lord has forgotten me.' Can a mother forget her infant, be without tenderness for the child of her womb? Even should she forget, I will never forget you" (49:14-15).

He has to convince the people that God is redeeming them, using Cyrus as his instrument. Therefore, he proclaims that the Jewish God is beyond comparison with any other gods, such as the Babylonian's Marduk: "I am God, there is no other; I am God, there is none like me" (46:9).

The Jewish God is the creator and lord of history: "It was I who made the earth and created mankind upon it; it was my hands that stretched out the heavens; I gave the order to all their host" (45:12).

He is the creator and redeemer of Israel: "Thus says the Lord, the Holy One of Israel, his maker" (45:11) and "Thus says the Lord, your redeemer" (48:17).

He promised that those who return will "enter Zion singing, crowned with everlasting joy; they will meet with joy and gladness, sorrow and mourning will flee" (51:11).

Therefore, he implores, "Break out together in song, O ruins of Jerusalem! For the Lord comforts his people, he redeems Jerusalem" (52:9).

Finally, the prophet proclaims that God is sovereign over all nations: "The Lord has bared his arm in the sight of all the nations; all the ends of the earth will behold the salvation of our God" (52:10).

Second Isaiah also contains four "servant-of-the-Lord" oracles. The servant is either all Israel or the prophet and his disciples. The fourth of these oracles contains the suffering and triumph of the sinless servant who by his voluntary suffering atones for the sins of his people, and saves them from just punishment at the hands of God. Christians see this prophecy fulfilled by the suffering and death of Jesus Christ.

The Third Book of Isaiah

What we know as Third Isaiah (chapters 56-66) was written back in the land of Palestine. An unknown disciple of Second Isaiah attempts religious reform, saying that the Temple must be open to all people, even eunuchs and foreigners who had previously been barred.

Chapter 58 calls the people to "true fasting": "This is the fasting that I wish: releasing those bound unjustly, untying the thongs of the yoke; setting free the oppressed, breaking every yoke; sharing your bread with the hungry, sheltering the oppressed and the homeless; clothing the naked when you see them, and not turning your back on your own" (58:6-7).

In chapter 60 the author prophesies the "glory of the New Zion," saying that the wealth of nations will be brought: "Caravans of camels shall fill you, dromedaries from Midian and Ephah; all from Sheba shall come bearing gold and frankincense, and proclaiming the praises of the Lord" (60:6). The Catholic Church uses this and other verses in this chapter on the feast of the Epiphany.

Chapter 61 begins with the words that Jesus read in the synagogue in Nazareth when he announced his mission: "The Spirit of the Lord is upon me, because he has anointed me to bring glad tidings to the poor. He has sent me to proclaim liberty to captives and recovery of sight to the blind, to let the oppressed go free, and to proclaim a year acceptable to the Lord" (Lk 4:18-19).

The book ends with a message of universal salvation, for Jew and Gentile alike.

15

THE BOOKS OF JEREMIAH, LAMENTATIONS AND BARUCH

Isaiah, Jeremiah and Ezekiel are considered the major prophets, mainly because of the length of their books. I will not, though, devote as much space to the latter two as I did to Isaiah.

I'm including Lamentations with Jeremiah because it was originally believed that he wrote the Lamentations, and Baruch was closely associated with Jeremiah because he was his secretary, although he didn't write the entire book. The three books are so closely related that the Council of Trent, when it listed the inspired books of the Old Testament, linked Lamentations with Jeremiah and said only "Jeremiah with Baruch."

Jeremiah was a fascinating man. *The Catholic Study Bible* calls him a type and model of Jesus Christ and says that it's not surprising that, when Jesus asked his apostles who people said that he was, some said Jeremiah.

Here are only some of the similarities between Jeremiah and Jesus: They were both confirmed in grace from their mothers' wombs, unmarried, hounded by hometown citizens, wept over Jerusalem, called the Temple "a den of thieves," met secretly with those who believed, and foresaw a new covenant.

The Book of Jeremiah includes biography, history and prophecy. Jeremiah was called to be a prophet when he was young, during the reign of King Josiah, whose reform of Judaism Jeremiah supported. When idolatry reappeared after Josiah's death and Jehoiachin became king, Jeremiah opposed it with strong prophecies about what would happen to the country. For his troubles, he suffered arrest, imprisonment and public disgrace.

After Babylon conquered Jerusalem the first time and took Jehoiachin in exile, Jeremiah counseled King Zedekiah, trying to prevent him from revolting against Babylon. But, of course, Zedekiah did revolt and Nebuchadnezzar destroyed Jerusalem, leading most of its citizens to Babylon.

Jeremiah, though, was left behind amidst the ruins. He wrote letters to the Jews in Babylon urging them to build houses, plant gardens, marry and raise families, because someday they would return to Jerusalem. Then he was forced into exile in Egypt and tradition has it that he was murdered by his own countrymen.

Thanks to his secretary Baruch, Jeremiah's influence grew after his death and can be seen in Ezekiel, some of the psalms, and Second Isaiah. His oracles contain sublime teachings. The book ends with an historical appendix.

The Book of Lamentations contains five lamentations over the fall of Jerusalem. Jewish Bibles place them with four other liturgical books (Ruth, Song of Songs, Ecclesiastes, and Esther) in a separate section called *Megilloth* or Scrolls, which are unrolled for special feasts.

You cannot tell it from the English translation, but the lamentations use poetic structures. The first four poems use the acrostic arrangement with the first letters of the stanzas following the Hebrew alphabet in order.

The first lamentation begins with the sorrow of the author when he sees the ruined city. Then Jerusalem itself confesses its sins, hopes and anger. The second lamentation lays the devastated city before God. The third is an individual cry of sorrow. The fourth tells of the end of nobles and children, has a meditation on Jerusalem, puts the responsibility on religious leaders, and curses the enemy. The fifth asks the Lord to remember.

The Book of Baruch is one of those books that was not accepted by the Jews as canonical, and, therefore, it also is not part of most Protestant Bibles. It consists of five compositions, the first and last in prose and the others in poetic form.

The first composition is a lengthy prayer of the exiles, attributed to Baruch but actually written much later by an unknown writer who reflected on the circumstances of the exiles in Babylon as he knew them from the Book of Jeremiah. It includes a confession of guilt and a plea for deliverance.

That's followed by a hymn of praise of Wisdom, extolling the law of Moses. Then Jerusalem is portrayed as the solicitous mother of the exiles who is assured by God that her children will be restored to her.

The final chapter in the book purports to be a letter from the prophet Jeremiah warning the exiles against idolatry while waiting patiently for the time that they will be able to return to Palestine.

16

THE BOOK OF EZEKIEL

As I mentioned before, Isaiah, Jeremiah and Ezekiel are considered the major prophets because of the length of their books, which is why I'm devoting separate chapters to them.

Ezekiel was the first prophet to prophesy outside the Holy Land. He was one of the 10,000 people exiled from Jerusalem to Babylon by Nebuchadnezzar in 597 B.C., after the Babylonians (also known as the Chaldeans) conquered Jerusalem the first time.

He apparently had a large following among the exiles. He began his prophecies about four years after his exile, in 593 B.C., and continued until 571 B.C. Throughout the book, he writes in the first person, but it's not really an autobiography.

When Ezekiel and the other exiles arrived in Babylon, they were convinced that Jerusalem would be spared destruction. God told Ezekiel otherwise, so the first half of the book consists of Ezekiel's attempt to prepare his countrymen for Jerusalem's destruction.

Therefore, much as earlier prophets in Judah had done, the first part of the book consists of reproaches for Israel's past sins and predictions of further destruction. Those predictions came true when Nebuchadnezzar destroyed Jerusalem in 587 B.C.

The book begins with Ezekiel's call to become a prophet

with his vision of four living creatures (later identified as cheru-
bim) and God's throne in heaven. God gives him a scroll to eat
and then sends him out to speak God's words to the house of
Israel, knowing that they would refuse to listen to him.

During another vision, Ezekiel was transported to Jerusalem
where he witnessed the abominations in the Temple followed by
the destruction of Jerusalem.

Chapter 11 contains Ezekiel's first prophecy concerning a
new covenant that God would make with the exiles. God said
that he would gather them from the nations to which they had
been scattered and restore the land of Israel.

Unlike the former residents of Jerusalem, they would live
according to God's statutes and carry out his ordinances. "Thus
they shall be my people and I will be their God" (11:20).

In chapter 12, Ezekiel is told to act out a scene in which he
dug a hole in the city's wall and left like an exile. When asked
what he was doing, he said that he was a sign to them, that the
people in Jerusalem would be exiled, including King Zedekiah,
who would be blinded before being taken to Babylon.

Jumping to chapter 16, we have an allegory about Jerusalem
which, although richly gifted by God, flaunted herself as a prostitute. It's another prediction of Jerusalem's destruction.

Chapter 18 is a disputation on personal responsibility. Ezekiel says that no longer would a son be charged for something
his father did, or the father for what his son did: "The virtuous
man's virtue shall be his own, as the wicked man's wickedness
shall be his" (18:20).

The restoration of Jerusalem

After the destruction of Jerusalem, Ezekiel's visions and prophecies are focused on the restoration of Judah. Chapters 25-32 are oracles against Israel's neighbors. Chapter 34 contains the parable of the shepherds. The idea of kings as shepherds was hardly new to Ezekiel. It was also found in the books of Samuel, Micah and Jeremiah. Of course, Jesus referred to himself as the Good Shepherd.

Ezekiel says that God himself would pasture his sheep, bringing them from the foreign lands and back to Israel. Furthermore, God said, he would appoint his servant David to pasture his sheep, a prophecy of a messianic king who would rule over the restored Israel.

Chapter 36 is another prophecy concerning the restoration of Israel. It's somewhat repetitious, but here God says that he wasn't going to restore Israel for Israel's sake but rather "for the sake of my holy name, which you profaned among the nations to which you came" (verse 22).

The first fourteen verses of chapter 37 are the well-known vision of the dry bones that inspired the song "Dem Dry Bones." It's a prediction of the restoration of Israel under the figure of a resurrection from the dead as the bones come together and are then covered with skin. It should not, though, be seen as a prediction of the final resurrection.

God said that he would put his spirit into those dry bones, which stood for the house of Israel: "I will put my spirit in you that you may live, and I will settle you upon your land; thus you shall know that I am the Lord. I have promised, and I will do it, says the Lord" (verse 14).

In the second fourteen verses of chapter 37 (15 to 28), Ezekiel is told to take two sticks. On one of them he is to write "Judah" and on the other "Israel." He is then to join them together so they form a single stick in his hand. Just so, God said, the old kingdoms of Judah and Israel will be joined together, never again to be divided.

God said, "My servant David shall be prince over them, and there shall be one shepherd for them all; they shall live by my statutes and carefully observe my decrees" (verse 24), again prophesying a messianic king.

Chapters 40-44 tell of Ezekiel's visions concerning the restoration of the Temple in Jerusalem. The first twelve verses of chapter 47 contain Ezekiel's vision of a wonderful and super-abundant stream flowing from the Temple, restoring to fertility land that is usually arid.

17

THE BOOK OF DANIEL

The Book of Daniel describes the life of some Jewish exiles in Babylon, which is why I'm discussing it at this point in the book. It's an ideal rather than a realistic picture, though, and the characters didn't really exist.

The stories about Daniel and his three companions are historical fiction, written to convey a religious message. The book was written in 165 B.C. during the persecution of Antiochus IV Epiphanes (whom we'll meet when we discuss the Books of Maccabees) to strengthen and comfort the Jewish people. There was a group of Jews who advocated nonviolent resistance to their oppressors. It was a member of this group who put the Book of Daniel together.

Instead of writing about his present time, the author placed Daniel and his three associates in Babylon during the Exile (587-538 B.C.) where they served a succession of three kings: Nebuchadnezzar, Belshazzar and Darius. (Historically, Belshazzar was never king and he wasn't the son of Nebuchadnezzar, as the book says, and Darius the Mede is unknown.)

The first six chapters tell stories about Daniel and his companions while the second six present Daniel's visions. The appendix, which is not included in the Jewish Bible because it exists only in Greek, has more stories. The stories might have originated during the Exile and been passed down through the centuries while the visions were written by the unknown author who published the book.

The author wanted to hold Daniel up as a model for youth. The stories, about heroic young Jews who were willing to die for their faith, taught readers that God would provide for the Jews the way to survive in a treacherous Gentile world – whether in sixth century B.C. Babylon or second century B.C. Jerusalem.

In the stories, Daniel is able to interpret dreams for Nebuchadnezzar and Belshazzar and thus distinguish himself. We also have the stories of Daniel in the lions' den and his three associates in the fiery furnace.

The second half of the book is apocalyptic, a series of visions promising deliverance and glory to the Jews. Christians are familiar with this type of literature because the Book of Revelation is apocalyptic; in fact, it was originally called The Apocalypse. It uses some of the same imagery as does chapter 7 of the Book of Daniel.

Apocalyptic literature uses symbols to present God's design for the world. In the Book of Daniel, he receives divine wisdom from the angel Gabriel, enabling him to understand the future. When interpreting Nebuchadnezzar's dream, he was able to predict future kingdoms (which the author knew succeeded the Babylonian Empire).

The author definitely believed in the resurrection of the dead. The book taught its readers not to live for this world but for "the kingdom of God," and it upheld the ideal of martyrdom. Jesus was to develop the theme of "the kingdom of God," first introduced by Daniel, in his parables.

Jesus also referred to himself as "Son of Man." It was the most characteristic way of referring to himself. In Daniel, "Son of Man" was a heavenly figure who came "on the clouds of heaven" and received from God "dominion, glory, and kingship" (7:13-14). Jesus quoted "the Son of Man coming in the clouds" during his trial before the Sanhedrin (Mk 13:26).

18

THE BOOK OF TOBIT

Before allowing the Jews to return to Judah from Babylon, which they do in the Books of Ezra and Nehemiah, I'm going to write about the Books of Tobit, Judith and Esther because the events in those books were supposed to have occurred before or during the exile in Babylon. They are listed in the Bible as historical books after Nehemiah, but they are not historical.

The Book of Tobit is a fascinating religious novel set after the fall of the Kingdom of Israel to the Assyrians in 721 B.C. The principal characters are Tobit, his son Tobiah, Sarah who has had seven husbands each of whom died on their wedding night, and the archangel Raphael.

I'll summarize the story, but I hope you'll read its fourteen chapters if you haven't done so before. It has long been a popular book among both Jews and Christians.

Tobit was a wealthy Israelite who was taken from Samaria to Nineveh by the Assyrians. We learn that he was a devout man, performing charitable acts and risking his life to bury the Israelites killed by Sennacherib. He once had to go into hiding when Sennacherib learned who was burying the dead.

But then he suffered financial reverses, contracted cataracts and eventually went blind. He prayed to God, begging him to let him die.

At the same time, in Ecbatana in Media, Sarah was despairing because of those seven husbands who were killed by the demon Asmodeus on their wedding nights. She, too, prayed for death.

God heard both prayers but did not grant them. Instead, he sent the archangel Raphael to heal both Tobit and Sarah.

Tobit remembered that he had left a large sum of money in Media, so he sent his son Tobiah to get it. Tobiah met Raphael, disguised as a man, and they traveled together. On the way, Tobiah was attacked by a large fish and Raphael told him to grab it, kill it, and remove its gall, heart and liver.

Arriving in Media, they stayed at the home of Raguel, Sarah's father, who was Tobiah's closest relative. At Raphael's urging, Tobiah married Sarah. During the wedding night, Tobiah used the fish's heart and liver to drive out Asmodeus.

After a wedding feast, Tobiah recovered Tobit's money and Tobiah, Sarah and Raphael made the return trip. On their arrival, Tobiah rubbed the fish's gall into Tobit's eyes and cured his blindness. Raphael revealed his true identity and returned to heaven. Then Tobit composed a lengthy joyful prayer.

Tobit died at age one hundred twelve, by which time Tobiah and Sarah had seven sons. Before he died, Tobit told Tobiah to leave Nineveh because the Lord was going to destroy the city. The whole family moved to Media where they learned later that Nineveh had been destroyed.

Within the story, the author included numerous maxims and teachings including fidelity to the law, reverence for the dead, the role of angels, honor towards parents, the purity of marriage, and the value of almsgiving, prayer and fasting.

19

THE BOOK OF JUDITH

The Book of Judith has long been a popular religious novel among artists and composers. Both Mozart and Beethoven wrote oratorios about Judith and she has often been depicted on canvas. The name "Judith" means "Jewess." The book was written as a pious reflection on God's providential care for the Jews and to give the Jews a heroine.

It appears to be history in the time of Nebuchadnezzar. But it says that he was king of Assyria when he was actually king of Babylon. The siege of the city of Bethulia, in the story, never happened.

According to the story, Holofernes, the commander of the armies of King Nebuchadnezzar, led an overwhelming force against the vassal states that refused to help in the Assyrian war against the Medes. The Jews resisted Holofernes at Bethulia. Holofernes laid siege to the town and, after 34 days, the Jews were ready to surrender.

Then Judith came to the rescue. She was a widow, "beautifully formed and lovely to behold" (8:7). But for three years and four months she had worn sackcloth and widow's clothing. She was known to be a God-fearing woman.

When she learned that the elders of Bethulia were ready to

surrender, she called them to her house and gave them a lengthy speech about how God was with the Jews as long as they didn't offend him. She asked them to let her out of the city and not to surrender for five days. The Lord would rescue Israel by her hand, she said.

Judith took off her widow's clothing and "made herself very beautiful, to captivate the eyes of all the men who should see her" (10:4). She and her maid made their way to the enemy camp. When she was captured, she asked to be taken to Holofernes, who was taken by her beauty. She praised King Nebuchadnezzar and said that she would help Holofernes defeat the Jews.

Holofernes gave her a room next to his and asked her to join him at table, but she insisted on eating only the provisions her maid had brought in a food pouch. She asked only to be permitted to go out each night to wash and say her prayers. Holofernes ordered his men not to hinder her coming and going.

On the fourth day, Holofernes gave a banquet and asked Judith to join him. She did, after putting on all her best clothing and jewelry. During the banquet Holofernes drank more wine than he had ever drunk before. Then the servants withdrew, leaving Holofernes and Judith alone.

Holofernes had passed out. Judith took his sword and, after saying a prayer, struck him twice in the neck, cutting off his head. She quickly took his head and passed it to her maid, who put it in her food pouch. Then the two women went out as they were accustomed to do for prayer. Unhindered by Holofernes' men, they made their way back to Bethulia.

With Holofernes dead, his army went into confusion and the Jews overwhelmed them.

20

THE BOOK OF ESTHER

Like Daniel, Tobit and Judith, the Book of Esther is another fictional book in the Old Testament. It's set in Persia (modern Iran) at the time of King Xerxes (485-464 B.C.), called King Ahasuerus in the book. It's an excellently written story and I encourage you to read it if you haven't done so. Here's a synopsis:

King Ahasuerus became displeased when his queen, Vashti, refused to come to a drunken banquet. He banished the queen and then searched the kingdom for beautiful virgins to replace her. Esther, an orphan who was being cared for by her uncle Mordecai, was one of the virgins brought to the royal court.

The book says that she "was beautifully formed and lovely to behold" (2:7). (If that sounds familiar, it's the same description given for the Jewish heroine Judith, whom I wrote about in the previous chapter.) The king chose Esther and made her queen in place of Vashti. On Mordecai's advice, she kept secret the fact that she was Jewish.

Haman was King Ahasuerus' second in command. When he passed on the street, all the people were to bow down to him. But Mordecai, as a good Jew, refused to bow down, keeping such homage for God alone. This angered Haman. He built a gibbet on which to hang Mordecai.

When he learned that Mordecai was a Jew, Haman told

King Ahasuerus that there were people in his kingdom who did not obey his laws. He proposed that all these people be rounded up for execution on a single day. The king issued the decree.

Mordecai put on sackcloth and ashes and walked through the city crying out loudly. Esther sent one of the eunuchs, Hathach, to learn why Mordecai was behaving like that. Mordecai told him what was about to happen to the Jews and asked Esther to appeal to the king.

Esther sent word for all the Jews to fast on her behalf. She and her maids also fasted and prayed for three days. Then she put aside her penitential garments and arrayed herself in her royal attire. Looking gorgeous, she approached the king, who sprang from the throne and welcomed her. What could he do for her, he asked.

Esther invited the king and Haman to a banquet. They accepted. During the banquet, Esther asked King Ahasuerus to spare her life and the lives of her people because an enemy was about to kill them.

"Who and where is the man who has dared to do this?", the king asked.

Esther replied, "The enemy oppressing us is this wicked Haman."

The king went into the garden in anger and Haman begged for his life. When the king returned, he found Haman on the couch with Esther. He ordered that Haman be hung on the gibbet he had prepared for Mordecai.

The decree against the Jews was rescinded. Then the Jews took revenge by killing a great number of their enemies. Mordecai replaced Haman as second in command.

Even though this book is fiction, the Jews celebrate these events each year on the feast of Purim.

21

THE BOOKS OF EZRA AND NEHEMIAH

Six chapters ago, we left the Judahites in exile in Babylon. They were taken there in 587 B.C., after the destruction of Jerusalem, including the Temple built by Solomon.

The Books of Ezra and Nehemiah, which were one book until St. Jerome translated the Old Testament, tell the story of the return of some of the Jews after King Cyrus of Persia, which had defeated Babylon, issued an edict in 538 B.C. encouraging the Jews to return to the land of Judah.

Obviously, not all the Jews were enthused about returning, or moving to Jerusalem for the first time, since the place was in ruins and the Jews had built their lives in Babylon during those 48 years.

Although Ezra precedes Nehemiah in the Bible, Nehemiah arrived in Jerusalem well before Ezra. He was in a group led by Zerubbabel and they were responsible for the rebuilding of Jerusalem and then the Temple.

The Book of Ezra shows the opposition to the rebuilding as the people of the land and the enemies of Judah tried to convince the Persians that the restoration of Jerusalem and the Temple was an act of political disloyalty. Their efforts failed, though, and the Temple was rebuilt in 515 B.C. It was not nearly as ornate as the one built by Solomon. That would have to await King Herod the Great.

Ezra doesn't appear in the Book of Ezra until chapter 7. He was a descendant of Aaron, the brother of Moses, a scribe who had become well versed in the law of Moses during the exile. When he arrived in Judah, it appears that the reconstruction of the city and its repopulation had already taken place.

Ezra focused on the establishment of the Torah as the constitution of the returnees. By their acceptance of the Torah, the people defined themselves as belonging to the Jewish community. In Nehemiah 8-10, Ezra read the law to the people, they confessed their failure to observe it in the past, and they agreed to live according to its precepts in the future.

Chapters 9 in both Ezra and Nehemiah contain the confession of the people. They are thought to be, originally, part of the same prayer. They recount the experience of the people from Abraham to the restoration and are considered to be one of the important creedal statements in the Old Testament.

A large part of both books deals with the problem of mixed marriages, those who married outside their religious community. Ezra recited a long penitential prayer on their behalf, speaking of the Jews as a "holy race" and accusing the Judahites of desecrating themselves with "the peoples of the land." Many Jewish men apparently divorced their non-Jewish wives.

Ezra thought that forbidding mixed marriages was essential to preserve the Jewish people because assimilation was a major threat, especially considering the small number of people who repopulated Jerusalem. The more the Jews associated with Gentiles the more was the likelihood that they would not remain ritually pure.

22

SIX MINOR PROPHETS

Six of the prophetic books in the Old Testament were written after the Babylonian exile: Haggai, Zechariah, Malachi, Joel, Obadiah and Jonah. All of them are short.

Haggai wrote his two chapters in 520 B.C. As we saw in the previous chapter, the Jews who returned to Judah were being blocked from rebuilding the Temple by Samaritans. Once permission was received from the Persians to build, Haggai encouraged them to do so.

He criticized the Jews for dwelling in their own houses while the Temple lay in ruins. Then Haggai prophesied that the future glory of the new Temple would surpass that of the old.

Zechariah's initial prophecy also dates to 520 B.C., and he, too, encouraged the returning exiles to rebuild the Temple. This book, fourteen chapters, contains eight symbolic visions, all promoting the work of the rebuilding. They are followed by a vision of a prosperous future during which nations will come to Judah in pilgrimage.

Chapters 9-14, though, come from a later period. They begin with the messianic vision of the coming of the Prince of Peace, including the appearance of a "just savior, meek, and riding on an ass, on a colt, the foal of an ass" (9:9). The New Testament evangelists see the fulfillment of this prophecy in Christ's entry into Jerusalem on Palm Sunday.

Malachi is the last book in the Christian Old Testament (but not in the Jewish canon; that's Chronicles). It was written shortly before Nehemiah's arrival in Jerusalem. In three chapters, it gives a picture of Jewish life between Haggai and the reforms of Ezra. He's tough on the religious indifference he saw.

Chapter 3 prophesies the day of the Lord, but first a fore-runner who will prepare the way: "Lo, I will send you Elijah, the prophet, before the day of the Lord comes" (3:23). Christ said that this prophecy was fulfilled in John the Baptist (Mt 17:10-13).

Joel also writes about the coming of the day of the Lord. His four chapters conclude with all nations gathered in the Valley of Jehoshaphat, where God judges them. But Jerusalem, he says, shall abide forever because "the Lord dwells in Zion" (4:21).

Obadiah is the shortest, but sternest, of the prophetic books – only twenty-one verses. It's a cry for vengeance against Edom because Edomites settled in southern Judah and were adversaries of the Jews who were returning from exile. Obadiah predicts that Judah and Israel will again form one nation and will occupy the lands of those who oppressed them.

The Book of Jonah, four chapters, was written after the exile. It's unique in the Bible because it tells the story of a dis-obedient prophet. When God told Jonah to go to Nineveh, he tried to flee and got on a ship going in the other direction. When a storm arose, he was cast overboard and swallowed by a great fish, where he remained for three days.

He finally went to Nineveh and preached. Then he was un-happy when the people repented and God didn't destroy the city.

23

THE BOOKS OF MACCABEES

The First and Second Books of Maccabees are not included in Jewish Bibles. Hebrew Bibles end with Chronicles even though the events in Ezra and Nehemiah happened later. However, the books were included in the Christian Old Testament when the Church selected the books in its canon and St. Jerome translated them.

The events in Ezra and Nehemiah occurred from the sixth to the fourth centuries B.C. In Maccabees we jump ahead to the second century B.C. Between those periods, the most important development was the conquering of most of the known world by Alexander the Great, and that's where First Maccabees starts.

Unlike the two books of Samuel, Kings and Chronicles, the two books of Maccabees are not a continuous narrative. They are independent accounts of some of the same events. First Maccabees tells the Jewish history from 175 B.C. to 134 B.C. while Second Maccabees is from 180 B.C. to 161 B.C.

Alexander the Great's successors took the culture of Greece to Jerusalem and environs, prohibiting Jewish religious practices and turning the Temple into a shrine to Zeus. Some Jews eagerly went along while others did not.

Eventually, practicing Jews were put to death. Chapter 6 of Second Maccabees tells the story of the martyrdom of an old man named Eleazar, killed for refusing to eat pork, and chapter 7 tells the inspiring story of the mother and her seven sons who were cruelly tortured and martyred.

Finally, Mattathias, of the priestly Hasmonean family, became infuriated when he witnessed a Jew offering sacrifice to the Greek gods. He killed the man and the king's messenger, and then rallied the people of Modein, where he lived, to follow him. They tore down pagan altars and forcibly circumcised any uncircumcised Jewish boys.

Mattathias died in 166 B.C. and was succeeded by his son Judas, called Maccabeus, derived from the Hebrew word for hammer. First Maccabees tells of his exploits in guerilla warfare, culminating in the purification of the Temple in Jerusalem, which Jews celebrate with the feast of Hanukkah.

The author makes it clear that Judas' victories came because of divine help, as he prayed before battles and praised God when he celebrated his victories.

In chapter 12 of Second Maccabees, Judas took up a collection that he sent to Jerusalem as an expiatory sacrifice for soldiers who died in battle while wearing amulets sacred to the idols of Jamnia. He did that "inasmuch as he had the resurrection of the dead in view" (verse 43). "Thus he made atonement for the dead that they might be freed from this sin" (verse 46).

After Judas was killed in battle, he was succeeded by his brother Jonathan. After Jonathan was assassinated, his brother Simon took over and became both secular leader and high priest. A period of peace ensued but then the aged Simon was murdered along with two of his sons. Another son, John Hyrcanus, continued the line.

The Hasmonean dynasty lasted about eighty years until the Roman general Pompey conquered Jerusalem in 63 B.C.

24

THE BOOK OF JOB

The Book of Job is the first of seven Wisdom Books in the Old Testament. These books, which date back to the tenth century B.C., were an attempt to answer some of the fundamental questions of life. The Book of Job is widely regarded as one of the literary masterpieces of all time.

Sometimes we hear that someone has "the patience of Job," meaning that she or he is an extremely patient person. I wonder if the person who coined that expression ever read past the second chapter of the Book of Job.

In the first two chapters of this folktale, Job indeed is patient. After God permits Satan to afflict him severely, Job says merely, "Naked I came from my mother's womb, and naked shall I go back again. The Lord gave and the Lord has taken away; blessed be the name of the Lord" (1:21). And later he says, "We accept good things from God; and should we not accept evil?" (2:10).

The first two chapters, though, are the prologue to the book, just as the last chapter, which tells of the restoration of Job's prosperity, is the epilogue. What makes this a literary masterpiece is the cycle of speeches from chapters 3 to 42. And there we find that Job is not patient at all. He curses the day he was born and longs for death to end his sufferings. He frequently cries out to God in complaint and blames God for allowing him to be afflicted even though he has always been a righteous man.

This is the age-old problem expressed in the modern book by Harold S. Kushner, *Why Do Bad Things Happen to Good People?* Why does God allow injustice to occur? Job's friends, who originally came to comfort him, are convinced that he must be guilty of some great wrong since his suffering is so intense, and they become annoyed with Job's protestations of his innocence.

Job pleads for God to explain why he has permitted this, and finally God answers. But not in the way Job wanted. God doesn't try to justify his actions; he doesn't answer the question "Why?" Rather he refers to his own omniscience and almighty power. He shows Job that happiness and success are not rewards for living righteously and neither are grief and failure punishments for evildoing.

This is enough for Job. He quickly recovers his attitude of humility and trust in God. In fact, his humility and trust are strengthened by the suffering he endured. Thus, over the 2,500 years since this book was written, this poor man has stood as proof that suffering is not a sign of wickedness.

From this book we learn that we do not know why bad things happen to good people and that innocent people can be afflicted for no apparent reason. Their sufferings are a test of their fidelity. They will be rewarded in the end but not necessarily in this life. Meanwhile, our human finite minds cannot understand the depths of God's divine omniscience and omnipotence.

25

THE BOOK OF PSALMS

Many Catholics have never been taught to appreciate the psalms. That's too bad because these ancient Jewish prayers remain essential to the life of the Church. Part of a psalm is included in almost every Mass. But too often those at Mass don't pray those psalms with any great devotion.

The psalms were the prayers Jesus prayed. As any good Jewish boy of his time, he probably knew most of the one hundred fifty psalms by heart. Even on the cross, he prayed Psalm 22, which begins, "My God, my God, why have you abandoned me?"

St. Thomas More loved the psalms. Some of them were part of his daily prayers, particularly the seven penitential psalms (6, 32, 38, 51, 102, 130 and 143). For night prayer with his family he chose Psalms 51, 25, 67 and 130, the *De Profundis*. Toward the end of his life he wrote an extended commentary on Psalm 91, and while in prison he collected verses from 31 psalms to form one powerful prayer he could pray in his cell. His last prayer was Psalm 51, the *Miserere*.

The *Catechism of the Catholic Church* calls the psalms "the masterwork of prayer in the Old Testament" (#2585). They were composed from the time of David until after the exile to Babylon but not as late as the Maccabean period.

Most of the psalms were composed for liturgical worship, although they are both personal and communal. Today, anyone who prays the Liturgy of the Hours prays almost all of the psalms over a four-week period, but some are prayed more often than others. The one prayed most frequently is Psalm 95, since it is the Invitatory Psalm, a call to praise God, the first prayer of each day.

Praise of God is the most common theme of the psalms. Indeed, the psalms were collected into five books of the Psalter, which means "Praises." But there are many other forms of prayer, too: lament, contrition, petition, thanksgiving. Some, too, reflect Jewish history and theology.

They usually are simple prayers and they sound spontaneous, but some are literary masterpieces, especially Psalm 119. By far the longest psalm in the Psalter, it has 176 verses. It is an acrostic: its 22 stanzas (of 8 verses each) are in the order of the Hebrew alphabet and each verse within a stanza starts with the same letter.

St. Ambrose wrote that "a psalm is a blessing on the lips of the people, praise of God, the assembly's homage, a general acclamation, a word that speaks for all, the voice of the Church, a confession of faith in song."

Some inappropriate psalms

Some of the psalms, however, might not be appropriate for your prayer life. The Church recognizes this in its Liturgy of the Hours. Someone who prays the entire Liturgy of the Hours over a four-week period (which the Church encourages all Catholics to do) will pray at least parts of 146 psalms. They will not pray Psalms 54, 58, 83 and 109.

It is precisely those psalms, plus portions of others, that

cause difficulties for some people. These psalms either contain accusations against God himself or curse antagonists. They contain such sentiments against their adversaries as, "O God, smash the teeth in their mouths," or, "Let them dissolve like a snail that oozes away" (Psalm 58), or, "My God, turn them into withered grass, into chaff flying before the wind" (Psalm 83), or, "May his children be fatherless, his wife, a widow. May his children be vagrant beggars, driven from their hovels. May no one treat him kindly or pity his fatherless children. May his posterity be destroyed, his name cease in the next generation" (Psalm 109). (It should be noted that Psalm 109 actually includes 14 verses of curses the one praying the psalms says his enemies say but then concludes, "May the Lord bring all this upon my accusers, upon those who speak evil against me.")

A few psalms seem to be worthy prayers but suddenly veer towards sentiments we would consider unworthy. Psalm 18, for example, is a long psalm of thanksgiving to God "my strength, my rock, my fortress, my savior." But while praising God for his help in battle, the one praying says, "I pursued and overtook my foes, never turning back till they were slain. I smote them so they could not rise; they fell beneath my feet.... They cried, but there was no one to save them; they cried to the Lord, but in vain. I crushed them fine as dust before the wind; trod them down like dirt in the streets."

Psalm 149 says that "God takes delight in his people.... Let the faithful rejoice in their glory," but then suddenly switches to, "With the praise of God in their mouths, and a two-edged sword in their hands, to bring retribution on the nations, punishment on the peoples."

These were apparently praiseworthy sentiments at the time

the psalms were written, but not today. What to do about them? I simply don't pray the offending verses; I skip over them. I conclude Psalm 149, for example, with "Let the faithful rejoice in their glory with the praise of God in their mouths."

Pray the psalms with which you're comfortable.

26

THE BOOK OF PROVERBS

Of the seven Wisdom Books, the Book of Proverbs is probably the one that best provides the guide for successful living that the ancient Israelites sought. But, of course, it isn't only the Israelites who struggle with questions about the meaning of life. Every culture does. So this book has universal appeal and significance.

The purpose of the Book of Proverbs, spelled out in the first chapter, is to teach wisdom: "That men may appreciate wisdom and discipline, may understand words of intelligence; may receive training in wise conduct, in what is right, just and honest" (1:2-3).

It then goes on, in 31 chapters, to present eight different collections of proverbs – usually short pithy sayings that express basic truths or practical precepts – applicable to people in various walks of life. Some are addressed to children, others to young men, and still others to citizens. The final chapter describes the ideal wife, whose "value is far beyond pearls" (31:10).

Many of the proverbs in these collections employ what is known as parallelism, usually two parts in a poetic construction. Sometimes the second part repeats the first part with a slight variation: "On the way of wisdom I direct you, I lead you on straightforward paths" (4:11). More often it contrasts ideas:

"Hatred stirs up disputes, but love covers all offenses" (10:12). And sometimes the second part advances the thought of the first part: "A cheerful glance brings joy to the heart; good news invigorates the bones" (15:30).

"The fear of the Lord is the beginning of knowledge" the book tells us in verse 7 of chapter 1. This concept is repeated in chapter 9, verse 10: "The beginning of wisdom is the fear of the Lord." This fear is a reverence and awe of God because of his sovereignty, goodness and justice. Besides being the beginning of wisdom and knowledge, this "fear" is also the foundation of religion.

The authors of these collections of proverbs believed that God created an order in nature and, if we could discern how that order operated and managed our lives accordingly, we would achieve wisdom, live successful lives, and find happiness.

The cultivation of virtue was seen as an important part of achieving wisdom and happiness. Discipline and self-control were seen as essential, and honesty, diligence, docility and humility were considered necessary for a good reputation.

Chapter 5 is a warning to young men against adultery and the seduction of women. It apparently was not deemed necessary to warn young women since, in a patriarchal society, they were kept in seclusion to guarantee their fidelity and only seductresses had freedom of movement.

The Book of Proverbs doesn't seem popular today, but there's a great deal of wisdom in this book written some 2,500 years ago.

27

THE BOOK OF ECCLESIASTES

Of the seven Wisdom Books of the Old Testament, the one that I've often questioned is not the Song of Songs, which I'll discuss in the next chapter, but Ecclesiastes. I dislike its negative and pessimistic viewpoint.

It's another book that searches for the ultimate meaning and purpose of human life. Its conclusion is that "all things are vanity." The author examines the things that humans usually search for – wisdom, pleasure, riches, renown – and finds them all lacking, "a chase after wind."

Although this book doesn't have the prestige that Psalms and Job have, most people are familiar with some of the expressions that come from Ecclesiastes, for example, "You can't take it with you," or, "There's nothing new under the sun" (1:9).

Most of us are also familiar with this passage: "There is an appointed time for everything, and a time for every affair under the heavens. A time to be born, and a time to die; a time to plant, and a time to uproot the plant; a time to kill, and a time to heal; … a time to weep, and a time to laugh; … a time to love, and a time to hate; a time of war, and a time of peace" (3:1-8).

The title Ecclesiastes is the Greek translation of the Hebrew name Qoheleth. The first verse identifies the speaker as "David's son, Qoheleth, king in Jerusalem." Since David didn't have a son named Qoheleth, the book was attributed to his son Solomon, known for his wisdom.

And what is Qoheleth's philosophy of life? It's summarized in the second verse: "Vanity of vanities! All things are vanity!" It's a Hebrew superlative expressing the supreme degree of futility and emptiness. Qoheleth has accomplished everything he set out to do and yet he says that nothing has any lasting significance. Everything seems futile.

He considered even wisdom as futile: "I said to myself, if the fool's lot is to befall me also, why then should I be wise? … Neither of the wise man nor of the fool will there be an abiding remembrance" (2:15-16).

But there is some positive advice. Qoheleth tells us to live for the moment, enjoy what we are doing because, like everything else in life, our pleasures are gifts from God. For him, the primary goal of life is living. Everything that promotes life is good while anything that doesn't promote life is "a chase after wind."

This philosophy is OK as far as it goes, but for Christians it doesn't go far enough. It's good to reject as the purpose or goal of life the pursuit of earthly pleasures and rewards of human accomplishment, but Qoheleth had no notion of everlasting life. There is the barest hint of a future life in Qoheleth's last word: "Fear God and keep his commandments, for this is man's all; because God will bring to judgment every work, with all its hidden qualities, whether good or bad" (12:13-14).

Qoheleth, though, didn't know what will happen after the judgment.

28

THE SONG OF SONGS

Perhaps the Song of Songs, a love poem full of sensuous imagery, doesn't seem to be an appropriate piece of literature to be in the Bible. But it does indeed follow the Book of Ecclesiastes.

Scholars have long speculated about why a poem about erotic love would be part of the Bible. But it was included in the Jewish canon, is read by Jews on the last day of Passover, and parts of it are included in the Catholic Church's liturgy, especially on Marian feasts.

As *The Catholic Study Bible* tells us, there are four ways of interpreting it: literal, dramatic, cultic and allegorical. In its literal interpretation, it is simply a collection of love poems that celebrate the passion of human love. Perhaps they began as Judean wedding songs that celebrated a fundamental human emotion – erotic love.

But people have looked for more than that. The dramatic interpretation goes back at least as far as the Christian theologian Origen, who said that it was a wedding poem written in dramatic form by Solomon. The fact that there is no narrative, only speeches, supports this interpretation. On the other hand, there is no dramatic development, no story line or character development.

So what if it was originally a liturgical reenactment of a drama that takes place in nature each spring – the cultic interpretation? Those who support this possibility note a well-known fertility myth in the ancient Near East: The great god (Baal for Canaanites or Tammuz for Babylonians) dies after the harvest and the fertility goddess (Anath or Ishtar) searches for him during the winter. Finally, with spring, she finds him, they are united, and the cycle of life continues.

Finally, there is the allegorical interpretation, the one most accepted by the Catholic Church. Just as Jewish commentators interpret the Song as symbolizing God's dealings with Israel, so Christians have long read it as a description of the mystical union of God and the individual soul. Some profound mystical theology, notably that of St. John of the Cross and St. Bernard, come from the allegorical interpretation of the Song of Songs.

Since this is one of the Wisdom Books, what does it teach us? In its literal interpretation, it simply but enthusiastically affirms that sexuality is one of God's great gifts to us. However, the sexual pleasure is pursued by the woman in the poems only within the context of a faithful and exclusive commitment.

The dramatic interpretation plays up the woman's unrelenting search, steadfast commitment, and fidelity as qualities to be admired and imitated.

The cultic interpretation, the dying/rising ritual, is that death does not have the final victory, that the love of the grieving goddess is enough to bring her lover back and to revitalize the earth.

And the allegorical approach gives us a way of understanding the nature of our relationship with God. God is not just an impassive creator or avenging judge, but a passionate lover who ardently desires union with us.

29

THE BOOK OF WISDOM

The Book of Wisdom is one of the Old Testament books that is actually more revered by Catholics than by Jews or Protestants. It is part of the Catholic Bible but not one of the Jewish canonical books because it was written in Greek rather than Hebrew, and Protestants accepted in their Old Testament only the books accepted by the Jews as canonical.

The author of the Book of Wisdom wrote in Greek because that was the prevailing literary language when he wrote it about 100 years before the coming of Christ. (That's also why the New Testament was written in Greek.) A large colony of Jews who lived in Alexandria, Egypt spoke Greek, and that's where this book was written.

Although not all of this book seems to apply directly to Catholics, especially praise of the wisdom of Solomon and a recounting of the events of the Exodus, the first ten chapters form a preparation for the fuller teachings of Christ and his Church. Many sections are used by the Church in its liturgy.

For example, one of the first biblical readings at funeral Masses comes from this book: "The souls of the just are in the hand of God, and no torment shall touch them," etc. (3:1-8). And Solomon's eloquent prayer for wisdom (9:1-6, 9-11) is included in morning prayer in the Liturgy of the Hours on Saturdays once a month. More readings from the Book of Wisdom are included in the Office of Readings during the Thirtieth Week of Ordinary Time.

The main theme of the book, naturally, is the praise of wisdom. As in other of the Wisdom Books, wisdom is depicted as a woman. In the patriarchal male-preferred society in which it was written, it is understandable that man's most desirable possession would be personified as a woman. It is also possible that Israelite ancestors believed in a goddess of wisdom.

Chapter 8 shows how wisdom embodies all the other virtues: "For she (wisdom) teaches moderation and prudence, justice and fortitude, and nothing in life is more useful for men than these" (8:7). Today we know those as the cardinal virtues.

For the first time in Jewish literature, the Book of Wisdom introduces the Greek concept of a soul, as in the funeral Mass reading.

The author of Wisdom agrees with other Wisdom Books (Job and Ecclesiastes) that virtue is not always rewarded in this life, nor is evil punished. There are sections on suffering, childlessness, early death, and the final judgment of both the wicked and the virtuous. After the judgment, the just will live forever, the author says. They "shall receive the splendid crown, the beauteous diadem, from the hand of the Lord" (5:16).

30

THE BOOK OF SIRACH

The Book of Sirach has something in common with the Book of Wisdom that I wrote about in the previous chapter: both were not accepted by the Jews as canonical. It's not clear why Sirach wasn't accepted. Perhaps it was because the translation that has come down to us is in Greek. But the original was in Hebrew. However, copies of the Hebrew version weren't discovered until 1896 and later.

Or, more likely, it was because the author had views that agreed with the Sadducees and it was the Pharisees who decided on the Jewish canon late in the first century.

Sirach was the name of the grandfather of the author, Jesus Ben Sira. The translation was done by his grandson, who also wrote a foreword in which he explained why he thought it important to translate the book and preserve his grandfather's wisdom.

It was written between 200 and 175 B.C., a period of time when Greek culture had permeated the entire Middle East and many Jews had abandoned their traditions, as we saw when I wrote about the Books of Maccabees.

Ben Sira, therefore, was writing to the Jews of his day to convince them that real wisdom was not to be found in the pagan philosophy of the Greeks but in Israel's traditions. He meant to write a comprehensive book of instruction and guidance for every circumstance of life.

The result was a collection of proverbs written as a series of essays. It resembles the Book of Proverbs more than any other book of the Bible.

Modern women won't think much of some of Ben Sira's purported wisdom. If they want to protest any book of the Bible, this is the one. Ben Sira blamed women for sin and death: "In woman was sin's beginning, and because of her we all die" (25:23).

He not only expected women to be submissive to their husbands but advocated punishment, including divorce, if they did not obey: "Be not indulgent to an erring wife. If she walks not by your side, cut her away from you" (25:24-25).

Like the Sadducees of Jesus' time, Ben Sira rejected any idea of life after death. He counseled moderation in grief when someone dies – one or two days – and then, "Turn not your thoughts to him again; cease to recall him; think rather of the end. Recall him not, for there is no hope of his return; it will not help him, but will do you harm" (38:20-21).

Despite some of this dubious wisdom, parts of the Book of Sirach have influenced both Judaism and Christianity. A scroll of Sirach was found among the Dead Sea Scrolls, evidence that it was considered Scripture by the Jews of Qumran.

Scholars find parallels between directives in Sirach and those in the Letter of James. Early Christian theologians such as Cyprian, Jerome and Clement of Alexandria quoted Sirach, and passages continue to be used extensively in our liturgies. Ben Sira continues to exhort us to maintain our traditional religious values in a godless culture.

ST PAULS

This book was produced by ST PAULS, the publish-
ing house operated by the Society of St. Paul, an
international religious congregation of priests and
brothers dedicated to serving the Church through the
communications media.

For information regarding this and associated minis-
tries of the Pauline Family of Congregations, write
to the Vocation Director, Society of St. Paul, 2187
Victory Blvd., Staten Island, New York 10314-6603.
Phone us at 718 865-8844.

E-mail: vocation@stpauls.us
www.vocationoffice.org

That the Word of God be everywhere known and loved.